NOBODY LOOK AT THIS BOOK
FOR 400 YEARS

NEIL'S BOOK OF THE DEAD

NIGEL PLANER
AND
TERENCE BLACKER

Harmony Books/New York

*Published in the United States in 1985 by
Harmony Books, a division of
Crown Publishers, Inc., 225 Park Avenue South,
New York, New York 10003
and simultaneously in Canada by
General Publishing Company Limited.*

*HARMONY and colophon are trademarks of
Crown Publishers, Inc.
Originally published in Great Britain by
Pavilion Books Limited.
Manufactured in Great Britain.*

Library of Congress Cataloging-in-Publication Data

Planer, Nigel.
  Neil's Book of the dead.
  1. English wit and humor. I. Blacker, Terence.
  II. Title.
  PN6175.P56 1986   828'.91407   85-14100
  ISBN 0-517-55964-1 (pbk.)

10   9   8   7   6   5   4   3   2   1

First American Edition

> ### AN APOLOGY
> Look, I'm sorry about this book, okay?

A Message to the World

I leave this Book of the Dead to:

~ the birds, the trees, the joyous overflowing the infinite beauty of oneness, big Rizla greens, the pyramids, Glastonbury, Dr Strangely Strange, the hills, the waves, the universe, Everything except bogies.

~ the police, the social workers, tutors, doctors, surgeons, ear nose and throat specialists and all other pigs. I love you.

~ My so-called father who, eversince I freaked out my so called family by dropping some so-called bad acid during Christmas '79, has freaked me out whenever I ring home for bread by saying "sliced or unsliced, Neil?" Heavy humour trip, Dad. Ha fucking ha. You asked for this one.

LISTEN to the sound of fishes going to bed. SEE music in the cider apple of your eye.
TAKE TIME to smell the flowers.

Goodbye.

neil

PS This is a suicide note by the way. Do not read it before I have actually killed myself. Goodbye.

mystical Prologue

People never listen to me and they're going to feel really bad when they find this book in four hundred years' time and discover all the shit I've been through and what a totally beautiful mind was snapped off in its prime.

ALL THE THINGS THAT ARE REALLY IMPORTANT TO ME ARE IN THESE PAGES.

I've put in everything I found when I was cleaning out my room before the Final Act, except the things that were too big to fit in like my duvet, which has been programmed to self-destruct when I reach my Goal.

THIS BOOK IS THE ONLY LUGGAGE I'M GOING TO NEED AS I GO THROUGH THE DEPARTURE GATES OF REALITY.

Once through those gates, I can travel light, past the security guards of perception, with no hassles at the customs check of earthly desires, and float freely up the steps of illusion on to that other plane.

I'M OFF NOW.

But that doesn't mean off like dead. Because a *Book of the Dead* isn't about death – it's really a Book of Life. Well, maybe there's one or two dead people in it, but it's really about my life, my quest through the beautiful jungle of my mind.

THIS BOOK WILL TAKE YOU THROUGH THE THIRTEEN MYSTIC STAGES, OR 'BOBOS', I WENT THROUGH TO GET WHERE I AM NOW (OR RATHER WHERE I WAS FOUR HUNDRED YEARS AGO).

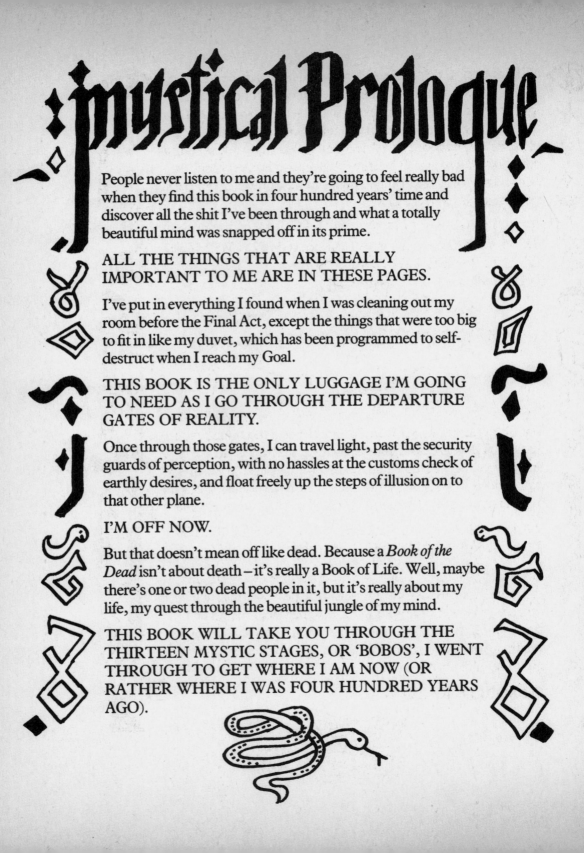

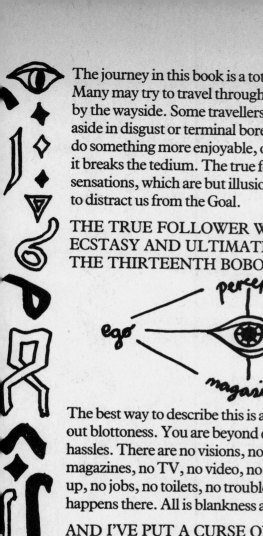

The journey in this book is a total mind and body experience. Many may try to travel through the bobos but end up falling by the wayside. Some travellers will cast their *Book of the Dead* aside in disgust or terminal boredom. Some will be tempted to do something more enjoyable, or even less enjoyable so long as it breaks the tedium. The true follower will ignore these sensations, which are but illusions, games thrown in our path to distract us from the Goal.

THE TRUE FOLLOWER WILL DISCOVER ECSTASY AND ULTIMATE ENLIGHTENMENT IN THE THIRTEENTH BOBO.

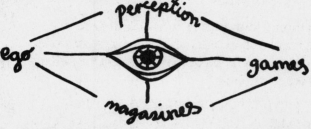

The best way to describe this is as a state of complete blissed out blottoness. You are beyond ego, beyond thought, beyond hassles. There are no visions, no words, no smells, no magazines, no TV, no video, no muesli, no pigs, no washing-up, no jobs, no toilets, no troubles, no toilet troubles. Not a lot happens there. All is blankness and all is truth. It's really nice.

AND I'VE PUT A CURSE ON IT SO DON'T READ IT FOR FOUR HUNDRED YEARS.

Books of the Dead are heavy magic so no one better read this until the year 2384 which, numerologically speaking, will be when people will have got their heads together enough to understand this book. Until then, I've cursed it and, if you're reading these words *before* midnight on 1st January 2384, you could be in really big trouble.

SO BOLLOCKS TO YOU.

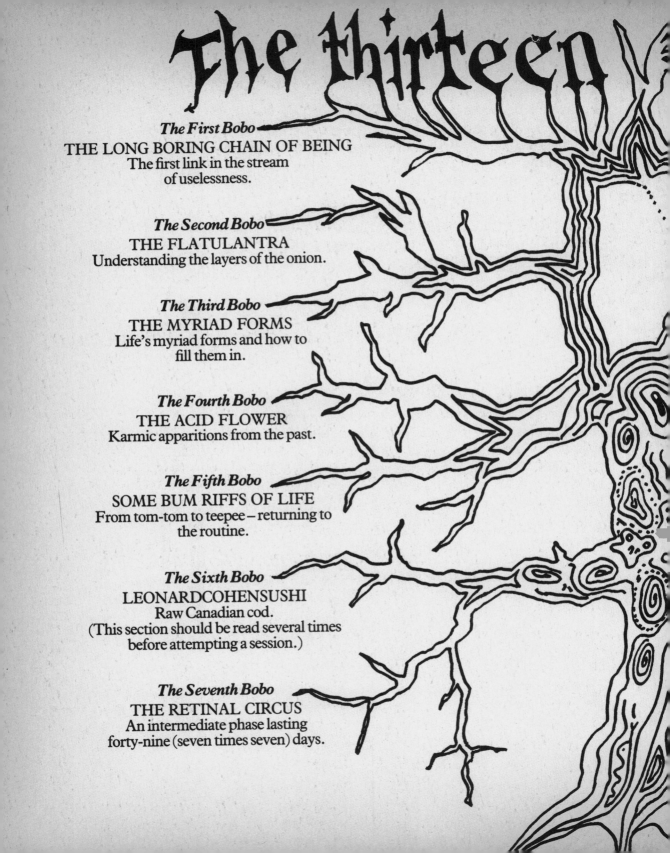

The thirteen

The First Bobo
THE LONG BORING CHAIN OF BEING
The first link in the stream
of uselessness.

The Second Bobo
THE FLATULANTRA
Understanding the layers of the onion.

The Third Bobo
THE MYRIAD FORMS
Life's myriad forms and how to
fill them in.

The Fourth Bobo
THE ACID FLOWER
Karmic apparitions from the past.

The Fifth Bobo
SOME BUM RIFFS OF LIFE
From tom-tom to teepee – returning to
the routine.

The Sixth Bobo
LEONARDCOHENSUSHI
Raw Canadian cod.
(This section should be read several times
before attempting a session.)

The Seventh Bobo
THE RETINAL CIRCUS
An intermediate phase lasting
forty-nine (seven times seven) days.

mystic bobos

The Eighth Bobo

EXTERNAL GAME REALITY
The diceman. Hallucinations. Go back two
squares before taking another turn.

The Ninth Bobo

THE BLAST OF SWOONING
Disease. Hardship. Mayhem.
Natural disaster. Destruction. Well scary.

The Tenth Bobo

THE WHEEL OF PERFECT PLEASURE
The bag of fulfilment. Full erotic
self-realization in a jiffy.

The Eleventh Bobo

BEYOND BOREDOM
The negation of the negation.
The unravelling of the unravelling.
The un-ness of the oneness.

The Twelfth Bobo

GETTING YOUR OWN BACK
The ultimate goal. Everyone's going to
really hate it when I get to
this level.

The Thirteenth Bobo

HOLY SHIT
You're never going to believe this.
I really didn't think it was going to be
this good. Wow. Wave. Energy. Flow. I am. Matrix.
You're really missing out on something,
you know. No, really.

First Bobo

The Long Boring Chain of Being

HOW! GREAT MAN OF PEACE! WE UNDERSTAND!

A poem for the spirit of the Red Indian and the Great Outdoor.

At Otling Fayre
I did my hair
So I could be like you.
I didn't know
That henna's made
From mud and camel's poo.

* * * *

The rocks, the rain,
The trees, the plain
And puddles everywhere,
I didn't bring
My plastic thing
And waterlogged my hair.

* * * *

We saw a band
And all held hands,
It was a groovy place,
But afterwards
I hitch-hiked home
With shit all down my face.

* * * *

How! Great Man of Peace! We understand!
Wow! Great Man of Peace! Totally far out and amazing!

We came in awe
Of the Great Outdoor,
We came to give and share.
They hadn't dug
A toilet trench
So we did it anywhere.

* * * *

There were jugglers there
At this great Fayre,
Mushrooms and fairy rings.
A peace teepee
From CND
And chicks who'd painted their things.

* * * *

The food of the plain
Was roots and grain
With totally whole earth flour.
It was tough as a brick,
It tasted like sick,
And I chewed it for half an hour.

* * * *

How! Great Man of Peace! I understand!
Wow! Great Man of Peace! Let's all go fishing!

Like you, we're free,
In harmony
We roam along the trail.
We're into seals
And whole food meals
And we save the whale.

* * * *

The White Man came
You fought in vain
He took your squaws and home,
And now he grabs
Our squats and pads
Although a lot of heavy white men are
          actually women these days.

* * * *

The crow, the deer,
The grizzly bear,
The budgerigar so tame,
The mighty eagle,
The neighbour's beagle,
They're basically the same.

* * * *

How! Great Man of Peace! We understand!
Wow! Great Man of Peace! The answer is blowing in the wind!

At Otling Fayre,
We were all there
At the mightiest of gigs.
Maybe two —
Two hundred and fifty
And that's not counting the pigs.

* * * *

The sun went down
We sat around
In a very mellow mood.
So we got higher
And poked the fire
While the chicks just cooked the food.

* * * *

Like the Cherokee,
We will be free
To live our lives in peace.
Together smoke
And pass a toke
And I've completely forgotten what I was going to say now . . .

A History of the Planet Earth

and the events that really mattered but the breadheads have tried to cover up so they can continue to rule the world . . . . .

25,000 BC The earth was populated with heads and freaks and prehistoric animals just living in peace without any bread or power hassles or pollution.

17,050 BC A monkey threw a big bone up in the air in slow motion and it never came down.

10,000 BC It was probably about this time that the astronauts came down in their chariots and started laying a whole heavy breadhead trip on the world pretending to be humans only now we know they weren't but it's too late because they've infiltrated and now they're all really negative parents and MPs and social workers and they've all taken over and it's like too late. Oh wow.

0 BC Invention of straight religion and the whole heavy church *Stars on Sunday* and Father Christmas scene. Wars started about this time.

1,400 The first recorded bad trip. King Canute freaks out and tries to make the sea go the wrong way. All the breadheads laugh at him when it doesn't work.

A Cavalier

16-something The breadheads start getting really heavy and wear big steel hats and call themselves Roundheads and import tobacco and dissolve the monasteries and really hassle Guy Fawkes and burn him for doing, like, nothing and then just go too far and cut the king's head off just because he had long hair and was into having a good time.

1840 Columbus discovers that there's quite a big country that the breadheads haven't fucked up yet so he sends a shipload of hand-picked breadheads over to give the beautiful peace-loving Indians alcohol-addiction, VD or, if that doesn't work, violent death. When everyone is infected, drunk or dead, they call it America.

really short hair

A Roundhead

1850 Victorian values are invented and exported at rip-off prices.

1930 Gandhi sets up loving peace communes all over India, invents vegetarianism and has a go at the New Way of Sex. Freaks from Jarrow march in sympathy.

1932 My dad was born. The polar ice-caps start melting.

1939 The heavy war trip where a lot of parents and grandparents got killed and ones that weren't just go on about it like it was all this whole big deal when basically it was just a load of straights fighting one another which wouldn't have happened if enough freaks were around giving out flowers and explaining things in a perfectly logical way.

Reading

Glastonbury

Isle of Wight

Woodstock

1944 Someone splits an atom. Churchill says this is not the beginning of the beginning. It is not the end of the beginning. It is a riddle wrapped in an enigma wrapped in a mystery. It will fight them on the beaches. It will fight them in Piccadilly. It will never owe so much to so many by so few etc. etc. Everyone gets really bored and stops fighting just to shut him up.

1947 Donovan is born with flowers in his hair.

1953 My dad and my mum get married. The coldest winter in history of mankind.

An Alien

1966 Everyone is totally freaked out when Dylan plays electric guitar for the first time at the Isle of Wight and blows everyone's mind and they're all really stoned and freaking out and doing poos in the open and painting their bodies and not washing their hair and letting butterflies go in protest against Vietnam.

1967 The dawning of the Age of Aquarius.

1969 The dawning of the Age of the Breadhead.

1970 I try to go and see *Easy Rider* but I'm not allowed in because I'm too young.

1972 The Stones Altamont concert freaks out the breadheads and leads to Edward Kennedy driving his wife off the bridge at Watergate and forcing the arch-pig Nixon to resign.

William the Conqueror, a straightie

1973 I go through my political phase and send an acorn for world peace to Edward Heath. He doesn't even write to thank me.

1975 I lose my virginity – at least I thought I did, until someone told me it doesn't count unless you're doing it with someone else.

the first video satelite link-up.

1976 The breadheads really start fighting back now, and when Richard Branson cuts off his hair and gets into the whole Young Conservative scene, suddenly it's hip to be a breadhead and alternative's like a dirty word and the Conspiracy is in total control.

1979 Dry cleaning is invented. Four million people die from fumes inhaled when they walk past dry cleaning shops.

digital briefcase

Friendly Pig

1981 I go on a creative writing course at a monastery in Scotland and start on the first draft of my *Book of the Dead*.

1984 The Age of Aquarius finally dies and all music is made by computers. Politicians have expensive white teeth but never smile. Rainwater starts tasting like asbestos. Norman Tebbit is made Minister for Truth. Donovan becomes a scientologist. And, freakiest of all, George Orwell predicted *all* of this.

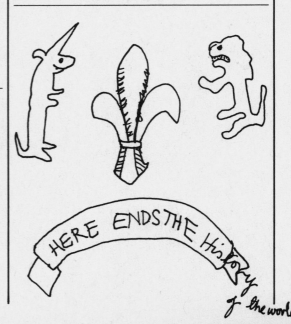

HERE ENDS THE History *of the world.*

HOMAGE TO HILLAGE

'It's all too much for me to take
The love that's skimming all around you
And all the world is just a cake
So take a piece but not too much.

Send mè on a silver sun
Til I know that I am free
Show me that I'm everywhere
But get me home for tea.'

(Except I just realised that this song
is by George Harrison!)

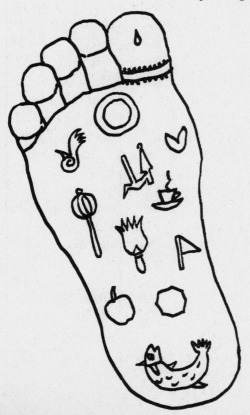

Total Nourishment Page

People all over the world think of lentils – if they think of lentils at all which is unlikely – as just a vegetable you sometimes find in soup. Well, all those people are wrong, right?

Lentils aren't just the most nutritious, healthy, friendly and totally balanced meal in the WHOLE UNIVERSE. They're more than that. Lentils are probably the most far out thing on the whole planet.
And that's why the lentil is often called 'a pulse' – because it has a totally unique vibe[1]! It is actually the *pulse of life*. So it's very important to touch them all the time with your fingertips.
In fact, lentils have amazing secret properties. For example: Certain tribes in New Guinea worship the lentil and they all live to be 150! The superpowers are involved in trying to utilize the lentil for intelligence purposes, like a cross between a dolphin and a microchip, except you wouldn't get a dolphin and microchip casserole, would you? We could insulate our houses with lentils – in fact, some people have made a start with a solidifying lentil soup called 'pebble-dash'. Last year, I lagged my attic with lentils and our electricity bill has been arriving late ever since. In the Third World, lentils could easily solve the insect problem – with organization, nations could rise up and stun locusts with them.

But the best thing we can do is to keep on using them in every possible way so that they don't disappear from the shops. I mean, I'm about the only person I know who's into lentils so I have to buy enough for at least a *hundred* people, just so that the grocer won't realise there's no demand and stop buying them.

---

[1] *Vibe* : what are vibes? Well you can't really talk about or say what vibes are, right, because whenever there's something that you *know* is happening but actually it's not happening, and everybody else says it's not happening, that's bad vibes. Good vibes haven't happened in this

My Lentil Recipe

1. Get a load of really good lentils.

2. Let them soak for a long time like until they're really bored and so are you. (The best place for soaking them is in the bath but don't forget to strain them afterwards to remove any unwanted grime or pubic hair.)

3. Cook them.

4. Eat them before anyone else throws them away or they go stale because they can really smell when they do that.

5. Fart a lot the next day.

Remember to talk to them a lot – they like that.

---

country for about ten years except sometimes when you're least expecting it, nothing might happen! But you'll know that there's an old vibe, like floating around and maybe it just landed in your karma[2] for a few moments and you'll say Vibe!

---

[2]*Karma*: Everybody's got their own personal karma. Sometimes people lose their karma or it gets stolen by gangs of tantric muggers, so you can get big pockets of karma accumulating in one place whilst somewhere else there isn't much. Karma has got to do with cause and effect; so no matter what it is you've done, like if you trod on an ant when you were a kid or just stubbed out a cigarette in someone else's pizza, your karma is going to pay you back eventually and one day you are bound to be trodden on by a giant bluebottle or drowned in a sea of mozzarella. So there is Good Karma[3] and Bad Karma.

---

[3] *Good karma*: This works the other way too; if you do something good like sitting in a park all day without blinking, or taking all the price labels off the food in a supermarket, or even just

like doing the washing up, your karma will be good later on in your life and you may be able to get free food in a supermarket, or someone else might do the washing up for you. Except this doesn't always work. I think I've accumulated a lot of bad karma, over the years, and I'm sure not all of it's mine. I bet you someone is offloading some of their bad karma into mine, or even stealing my good karma, like when your neighbours connect themselves to your electricity meter. Unless it all comes from one of my previous reincarnated[4] lives.

[4]*Reincarnation*: If your karma is very very bad, when you die you will get reincarnated as something much worse than you are now, to sort of pay you back for having such bad karma. So if you never did the washing up at all and were like really heavy and violent and aggressive in this life you might come back as a football or a doormat, just so you could see what it was like being kicked around and trodden on. I sometimes think I have been reincarnated as a doormat already. The problem with reincarnation is that, if you've got bad karma, reincarnation will make it worse and worse until you are just a piece of mould in the sink and, if you start off with Good Karma, reincarnation will just make it better and better until you are the most cosmic tantric[5] wizard in the universe. It's really unfair.

[5]*Tantric*: What is tantric? Well it comes from Tantra; Tantra is what wizards and gurus do instead of having heavy relationships and sexual hang-ups. The tantra of sex is when you learn how to release the sexual energy of kundalini the serpent which lives in the base of your spine and only comes out every now and then to give you a higher state of consciousness rather like herpes.[6]

[6]*Herpes*: Herpes is another energy form that lives in the base of your spine, but whereas kundalini goes upwards to your brain and totally freaks your higher centre, herpes comes out on the end of your cock (or you labia if you're, like, a chick) in the form of little white 'herps' and you've got to put salt on them until they go away again. One of the main symptoms of herpes is depression. Many famous poets, singers and artists have worked under its powerful influence and, in fact, some people say that the National Theatre building, London, and the Common Market were inspired by herpes. But anyway where was I? Oh yes, Tantra. Tantra comes from Tibet.[7]

[7]*Tibet*: is where the astronauts landed in 10,000 BC. Until about thirty years ago, Tibet was called the attic of the world because it was where all the dusty old books of wisdom were kept, but then in the so-called 'lagging offensive' the Chinese army came and threw out all the monks and priests. Recently they've started letting all the Tibetans back in, including, the Dalai Llama.[8]

[8]*The Dalai Llama*: The Dalai Llama is a sacred animal which the Tibetans worship. I've never been able to work out why they worship an animal that comes from South America, or how they used to get llamas over to Tibet thousands of years ago before modern boats and trains

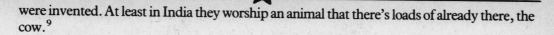

were invented. At least in India they worship an animal that there's loads of already there, the cow.[9]

[9]*Cows*: Cows are animals which make milk and moo, and have tongues as big as your arm. Cows usually have good vibes, although their karma is usually to end up between sesame buns underneath pickled gherkins. When I was in Glastonbury[10] I saw some cows which could stand sideways on hills.

[10]*Glastonbury* is like the centre of power where all the cosmic energy forces meet. I lost my Jim Morrison T-shirt there in 1979 so it must be pretty impregnated with power by now. All leylines[11] start and end at Glastonbury.

[11]*Leylines* are magic lines that join all the important mystic sites together. They are like cosmic motorways which you can hitch down to get to all the far out places, like all the stone circles like Stonehenge etc., and to all the festivals. Some people spend their summer holidays digging up leylines to see if they can find old relics and things of archaeological interest. These people are Cosmic Wankers.[12]

[12]*Cosmic Wanking* is like black holes in space. Nobody knows what goes on in the mind of a cosmic wanker but if you look between their eyes you can see an infinite number of other faces flash past in front of you, especially if you don't blink. (This is how we get the expression 'you two faced cosmic wanker'.) P.S. Doing this is like, quite dangerous and should not be done by anyone who is tripping.[13]

¹³*Tripping*: When you are tripping you are likely to see an infinite number of faces everywhere, not just on cosmic wankers. Most of your friends will look horrible to you because you will see right through them, so you must be careful not to bump into them. Tripping is something people do even though most of the time it is amazingly unpleasant. The most obvious ways of tripping are to take LSD, mescalin, peyote, or mushrooms. ¹⁴

---

¹⁴*Mushrooms*: Mushrooms have rights too! The way to get the best mushrooms is to find a wood miles away from anywhere and put up a tepee or a tarpaulin in a dark moist clearing in the wood right? And then sit there and watch and wait for the mushrooms to come to you. If you keep very still for a few days you will start to see them grow. Watch them grow close to you each day as you get more damp and mouldy. When they've nearly got to you, but just before they start actually growing on you, you've got to leap up and pick them all and put them in your basket. There is a danger in this, because if you leave it too long, or fall asleep at the wrong moment they will capture you and take you away which is like the heaviest trip of all time. I know because it happened to me right, and it took me three years to get out of a mushroom reality¹⁵ and back into a Neil one.

---

¹⁵*Reality*: Reality doesn't actually exist. Anybody who tries to tell you that it does exist is either just trying to freak you out, or might be an alien. ¹⁶

---

¹⁶*Aliens and Astronauts*: If you are an alien reading this you will know what you are so go on to the next bit without reading this bit. If you are not an alien or an astronaut, then watch out.

One good way to find out if someone is an alien or an astronaut is to give them this book and see if they skip this paragraph. Remember an alien or an astronaut can look quite normal even though somewhere on their bodies is a little plate which unscrews, where all the wires are. One of the best examples of the superhuman powers of an alien is Bruce Lee. [17]

---

[17]*Kung Fu and Martial Arts*: What's so brilliant about kung fu and other martial arts is that you can leap up in the air and nut someone in the face without any aggression or violence. The wise men of the East are allowed to break each other's bones and teeth and like cut each other into pieces and tear each other up and still be into love and peace. Most western people get heavy and hostile just shouting at each other and giving each other heart attacks, which is why some people started meditation. [18]

---

[18]*Meditation*: The whole idea of meditation is to sit down and not think about anything, not even think about not thinking about anything, until you're so bored that the blank wall you're staring at starts to get really interesting. The trouble with it is that there's always somebody who comes and laughs at you when you're trying to do it and then you start thinking about how much you hate them and then you've blown the whole thing, and then you get really angry and then you need to meditate more and the whole thing becomes just like a real bummer. [19]

---

[19]*A bummer*: A bummer is about the most down thing that can happen to you right? If you were trying to light a cigarette and your lips were really dry and they stuck to the filter but you didn't know they had so when you tried to take the ciggie out of your mouth it stayed there while your fingers slid down the shaft to the glowing end and you burnt your fingers, and then when you tried to take the cigarette out of your mouth properly it tore the skin on your lips and they started to bleed and the smoke from the ciggie went backwards up your nose and into your eyes, and then while you were looking for the antiseptic cream for your fingers and lips you'd come across the nail scissors and accidentally cut off your tongue, that would be a bummer. There are different sizes and types of bummers. Some are little and some are large. [20]

---

[20]*Little and Large*: Little and Large are two evil spirits who live in TV and radio waves. They get their evil way by making you feel as if you ought to be laughing and having fun, but you're not, but then no one else is either so really the whole thing is a bit of mind fuck. [21]

---

[21]*Mind fuck*: A mind fuck is when you don't understand what's going on, or even if anything is going on at all. Mind fucks happen a lot these days, as do refreaks. [23]

---

[23]*Refreak*: A refreak is when you get this sort of vibe$^{1/24}$ that reminds you of a vibe$^{1/24}$ you think you had once before but you can't remember when.

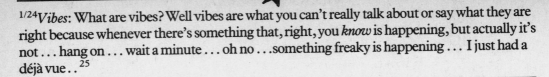

[1/24]*Vibes*: What are vibes? Well vibes are what you can't really talk about or say what they are right because whenever there's something that, right, you *know* is happening, but actually it's not . . . hang on . . . wait a minute . . . oh no . . .something freaky is happening . . . I just had a déjà vue . .[25]

[25]*Déjà vu* is when you get this sort of vibe[1/24/26] you think you had once before but can you remember when. Huh?

[1/24/26]*Vibes* What is going on? . . . Help! I think I've just got stuck on the long boring chain of being[27] again.

[27]*The Long Boring Chain of Being* is like when you keep saying the same things again and again, and people get even less interested in you than they normally are. No, but listen, I've got a really important one . . .

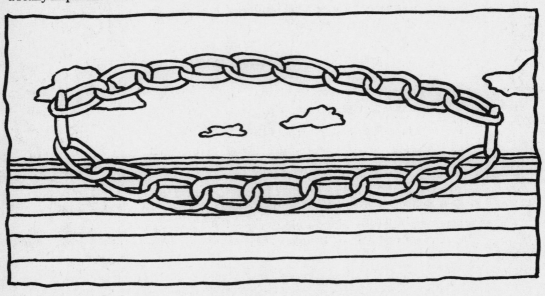

Neil Meal

I don't eat meat because you are what you eat
And I'd rather be a vegetable
Than a cow or a sheep.
Except I'm more of a cereal really
And probably there's no free gift in me either.

Personal Poem

Add your own words to make this poem personal to you.

Plodding along a secret lane,
Mud sticks, ankle pain,
Plodding helps to keep you sane,
But it's really uncomfortable in the rain.

Eating ice cream with a fork
Is really difficult, heavy work,
But not as disgusting as eating cold pork,
You'd be really stupid to eat blackboard chalk.

Writing one stupid verse a day
Is better than working without any pay
Or listening to Michael Jackson play,
But it stops you from (*Insert your own experience here*).

© neil

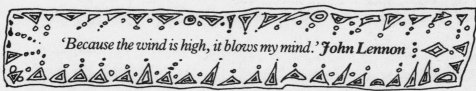

'*Because the wind is high, it blows my mind.*' **John Lennon**

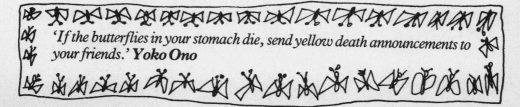

'*If the butterflies in your stomach die, send yellow death announcements to your friends.*' **Yoko Ono**

Did you know that, if you melt down all of Janis Joplin's albums and then throw them out of the window into a cold bath full of rainwater they make the mystic word of MALAMEQOOONKOITZ, which means 'I really am dead'?

Also that the colour of the cover of *Smash Hits, July 1967* which featured Janis Joplin on it was yellow?

And like yellow, or saffron, is the Buddhist colour of death?

And did you know that, if you burn *Smash Hits, July 1967* and look into the ashes, Janis Joplin turns into a piece of thin glowing black charcoal which gets carried on the wind and lands on the tail of a black cat that squeals and leaps up suddenly and goes down the garden path?

All this points to one incredible fact. Janis Joplin is actually dead! Heavy but true.

'So what?' you might say, 'so is Jim Morrison.' But you'd be wrong! Because I had a friend called Dave the Sparrow who told me what *really* happened.

When you're a big rock star and you've made five singles and loads of albums and you start to run out of inspiration, you get to this point where you have to decide whether to sell out or not. And to start making typical media-gonzo type music and wearing pink satin suits and things like that. Most rock stars do that because most rock stars are a sellout.

Anyway if you decide you don't want to sell out, you get put in touch with this special agency right called Abbey Death and General and they come round to your house in a suit (well only one of them wears the suit at a time) and they've got all these brochures of schemes of what you can do, if you pay the agency a regular fee by banker's order.

Basically you sign all these forms and they kill you, right, and then all your record royalties double and you get all this publicity and, if you've been in any films they all get put on telly again, and you don't have to write any more songs at all because you're dead, right?

Except you're not really dead at all, because the agency take you in disguise to this island called Death Rock Island (or Rock Death Island I can't remember which) and you can stay there. And all the famous rock stars live there, and nobody knows where it is, and when you get there you might bump into Buddy Holly playing space invaders, or you could go for breakfast in the canteen and find yourself in a queue between Brian Jones and John Belushi (sometimes they let film stars in too).

And all the rock stars who live there can do exactly what they want because they're all really rich because they've all become like, LEGENDS and there's as much dope there as you can take and all the time your record royalties are piling up. It's rather like the village in *The Prisoner* except it's full of international rock stars not sixties character actors.

Anyway, after you've been there a few years and you've got really bored with it and all your money's run out and most people in the real world have forgotten you except for your fan club and the people who make T-shirts, the agency run this second scheme and they recycle you back into the world in a new town with a new name.

So one of *your* best mates might in fact be Jimi Hendrix!

I saw Jim Morrison in a pub in Harrow a few months ago – he's a welder now called Roger Herdiman. Of course he denied that he was Jim Morrison, but then you have to, that's part of the whole scheme.

And this is the real reason why they won't open up Elvis's grave, right. Because, in fact, Elvis Presley is now an ice-cream salesman in Notting Hill Gate called Mike Mario.

Mama Cass

Vicky MacIntyre

Marc Bolan

Brian Chubb

Jim Morrison

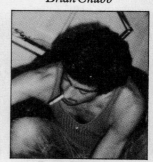
Roger Herdiman

Elvis Presley

Mike Mario

Second Bobo

The Flatulantra

By now, if your inward concentration is properly attuned, you will start to notice new, exciting things about your body and its magical organic functions.

Listen carefully to its secret messages and try to feel part of its essence, its fullness, its daily rhythms. Soon you will find you can go with it on an amazing journey out of the body, travelling upon a long golden stream.

As the out-of-body experience commences, remember to relax completely and let your mind go completely blank. Perhaps whistle softly to help your concentration. Aim carefully and just go with the flow.

If at this stage, the out-of-body experience causes a sharp, burning sensation, stop at once and call your alternative health centre.

Now you are no longer a solid mass but liquid, and travelling faster than you believed was possible. You are part of the Great Riddle of Life, the Golden Flow of Being.

You will find that you can grow in all sorts of unexpected directions. Play in rivulets. Try to reach the ceiling. Run down walls. Get absorbed in things.

Look around you. Look at yourself. Are you clear or murky? Your out-of-body appearance can have its own mystical significance, as you will see on this chart.

Flow of Being

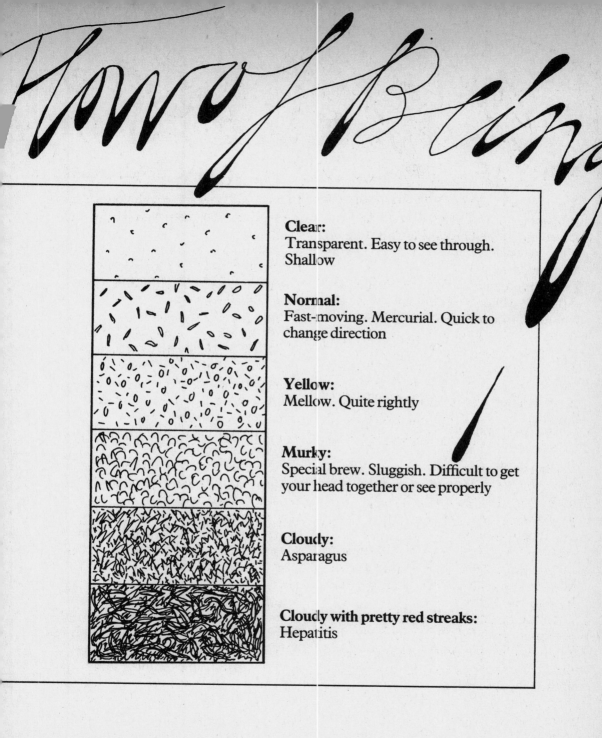

Clear:
Transparent. Easy to see through. Shallow

Normal:
Fast-moving. Mercurial. Quick to change direction

Yellow:
Mellow. Quite rightly

Murky:
Special brew. Sluggish. Difficult to get your head together or see properly

Cloudy:
Asparagus

Cloudy with pretty red streaks:
Hepatitis

HOW TO TURN YOUR BEDROOM INTO A SQUAT IF YOU'RE LIVING WITH YOUR Parents.

A guide for people who want to squat but aren't lucky enough to be totally independent and homeless

Getting In

Legally you can be thrown out of a squat if the pigs can prove that you used force to enter. So do *not* use a mallet or a chainsaw when approaching your bedroom. Look to see if all's clear, turn the handle and push the door. Do not act suspiciously – just walk straight into your room as if you were meant to be there. Alternatively you could just leave the door open for yourself the night before.

Setting up the squat

Now you are in there are a few things you must do straight away.

1. Smash all the lightbulbs.
2. Put patterned bedspreads all over the walls and ceiling to make the place feel more cramped and to create damp pockets of air against the walls and in all the corners.
3. Take your bedframe out from under your mattress and throw it out of the window. If the window was closed at the time, all the better – you can tape it up with a piece of cardboard later.
4. Put your mattress on the floor so you have to walk all over it every time you want to cross the room. If it gets a bit mildewy and mouldy under the mattress this is good, it will help to make the place smell right.
5. Take all your dirty washing out of the laundry bag and mix it in with any clean clothes you might have. Scatter them both on the floor.
6. Put some ashtrays on the floor. Do not scatter the ash as it builds up, just let it get trodden in gradually over the next few weeks in a natural organic way.
7. If you have a table, saw off the legs so that no one can be bothered to get up once they've sat down.

To put the final touches in, you will need:

a) a broken incense holder
b) a lot of old science fiction novels
c) a television set that doesn't work
d) a box of used matches
e) a very thin dog
f) a mono record player and one Led Zeppelin album which someone has stubbed a cigarette out on.

You are now a squatter

Invite all your friends round to help mess the place up and mope around. If they're bedroom squatters at their parents', agree to do the same for them some time. Or if you don't have any friends just go out on the street and say to passers-by, 'Hey, wanna come and mope around in my bedroom squat for a bit?'

Heat and Light

By now your parents will have disconnected your room so you will have to depend on an alternative energy supply. See illustration.

How to light a candle.

(A good way of getting the candle to stand up is to pour some of the soft wax from the top of the candle into the carpet, if you still have one, and then stand the candle in this as it solidifies.)

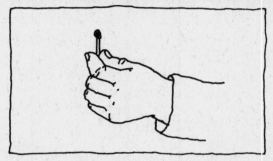

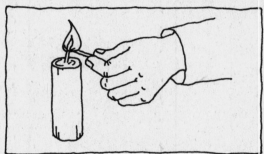

Food

Get a hunting party together and go on food expeditions late at night. Creep downstairs into the straights' kitchen and take everything you want from the fridge and cupboards and take it all back upstairs to your squat, not forgetting to take a tin-opener too. Do *not* have a fry-up in the kitchen since fatty smells and sizzling noises can really upset the straights and they might come downstairs in their pyjamas and spoil everything. (Don't worry about mugs and things, you will accumulate them as more and more people have coffee in your bedroom.)

You really are a squatter now

One last thing you could do is to look around your neighbourhood, in people's back yards and rubbish tips for any old broken bath tubs, radios and that don't work, bits of bannisters etc, and bring them all back and leave them around your parents' house to make the approach to your squat more acceptable. Happy squatting!

HOW TO TURN YOUR SQUAT BACK INTO A BEDROOM AGAIN BECAUSE PEOPLE KEPT TAKING advantage of you.

I mean, okay, fair enough the whole idea of a squat is to, like, share, but some people kept sharing all of my stuff and I never got to share any of theirs. Some people even started setting up their own alternative squat in my squat, and I know that really everything is collectively owned in a squat but someone ate all my organic maple syrup, and like I have to have that because I don't have white sugar any more, right? I mean the person who took it probably thought they'd just try it for a taste experience as a change but it's the only thing I can EAT, RIGHT?

1. Getting rid of everybody
I know this sounds heavy and I don't want to seem like a prison warden or a fascist dictator but the first thing to do is get a really good lock put on the door if you've still got a door. Two locks and a bolt is even better. Banham or Yale will do, and make sure that you're the only one who's got the key. Keys can make quite good medallions round your neck actually.

I mean, no one else turned their bedroom into a squat, they just left their bedrooms the same as before, *and* their mums even came in and did the hoovering once a week so why should they all end up squatting in *my* squat? I mean a squat's a squat right?

2. Redecorating
Realise that it's going to take more than one coat of paint to cover up all the graffitti on the walls. I mean I didn't even do all of it. Not even half of it really.

Spread ash thoroughly into every last inch of the carpet to make it all a uniform colour, or better still paint the carpet grey. Go and get the bed frame from where you left it in the back yard or on the street, and put it back under your mattress. However, if it is full of rainwater now and a bit warped, you may have to put all the old radios and science fiction novels and your mono record player under your mattress as a bed frame, which is really uncomfortable. Alternatively, try slinging up a hammock out of all the old bedspreads on the wall. Be careful when you get into the hammock that it's strong enough and that your weight doesn't pull any of the damp plaster off the walls. Oh no! If this does happen, your best bet is to hack all the plaster off the walls with a pick-axe and give your bedroom that sort of country brickwork look.

3. That's it really
Okay, so there's plaster and rubble all over the floor and the window's still broken and your mum and dad still haven't reconnected you, so it's very cold and draughty and completely dark, but at least no one else can rip it off, right?

'Maybe the other life won't have many good moments either, I know this one and I don't want it.' – **Leonard Cohen**

'Reading does a lot for your brain.' – **Paul Weller**

(And so does Glastonbury! – **Neil**)

'I feel very privileged to be able to fly round the world in search of myself, and I want to give something back by sharing my experience with others . . . Life is like hot sauce. As soon as you start enjoying it, it makes you cry.' – **Shirley Maclaine**

'You only know you haven't been there when you return from not being there . . . When the eagle flies it leaves no mark. That's what Krishnamurti says. We can dilute the memory of the present moment – with the girl last night or the fellow tomorrow. So we miss the moment, the one thing that's unique. It's a hobby of mine – seeing when I'm there and when I drift off.' – **Terence Stamp**

'Gosh, life is really too much.' – **Donovan**

'Our legs carry us forward through life.' – **Samuel Dunkell MD.** **Sleep Positions**

PARANOIA POSTCODES

Paranoia Postcodes
They watch you through TV
Helicopter surveillance
And thinking pills in your tea

Paranoia Postcodes
Addictive take-aways
A tunnel joining your toilet
To laboratories in Hayes

Paranoia Postcodes
A message in the yolk
And why do all the newscasters
Always end up with a joke???

THE SECRET LIFE OF RUBBER PLANTS

This is a picture of my rubber plant, Wayne.

*People all have the wrong idea about rubber plants
and in fact about all plants in general.*

Did you know that plants are more intelligent than dolphins? This has been proved by some scientists in California who did some tests which proved that all dolphins are interested in is jumping and sports and things whereas plants like to spend the time indoors thinking. And just because they are stay-at-homes and don't go out playing agressive macho games, people are more interested in dolphins than plants. Typical.

Anyway, these scientists discovered that plants can understand what you're saying and are aware of any bad vibes around and that they really like music and that if you talk to them and say nice things they grow better.

I always talk to Wayne, but he's been behaving really strangely the last few weeks. I think he's pissed off with me for some reason. Maybe it's because I haven't given him any bio-strath for two months or maybe it's because I broke off two of his leaves and put them in the oven and rolled them into a joint and smoked them when I was really desperate last Christmas. Anyway he hasn't been talking to me recently, he's been really sulky.

I hate that when your own rubber plant keeps secrets from you. I'm sure he gets into things when I'm not there that he doesn't tell me about.

Hey! . . . I just thought maybe that's what everyone means when they talk about the secret life of plants! Yeah!

WAYNE SETS OFF ON A Journey

Wayne embarks upon his quest
We hope you'll see him at his best
'I'm off to Mexico to take peyote'
Well don't forget your winter coaty!

Now as Wayne wanders through the dew
A Viking ship sails into view
And out jumps a Viking lad
'We'll take you there, we're not so bad!'

'We're not into rape and pillage
We like health food and Steve Hillage'
So Wayne gets in and in a sec
They are in Poxolpeteltec!

'First things first' says Wayne 'Let's score'
And knocks upon the nearest door
Inside a lizard bids them near
'Come in my boys, I've got the gear.'

The Secret Life of Rubber Plants
WAYNE MEETS A TALKING CACTUS

Says Viking Marty 'Will we get busted?'
'Can this lizard here be trusted?'
And on Wayne's sleeve he gently tugs
But Wayne's too busy taking drugs

Then everything begins to hum
And weird hallucinations come
And life becomes an endless void
Enough to make Wayne paranoid

Just then a cactus man appears
And says 'That's it for now, so cheers!'
'We wouldn't want you to OD'
'You must be home in time for tea'

The ship is waiting on the shore
And drops Wayne off right at his door
'Oh come with us' says Viking Marty
'Fuck off' says Wayne, 'I'm off to party.'

The Secret Life of Rubber Plants
WAYNE DIGS JAH MUSIC.

'A drink, you bums' is Wayne's first cry.
But he's too late, the party's dry.
Let's dance he calls, 'This party's dead.'
And jives on to the flower bed.

The disco beat exhausts young Wayne
And makes a buzzing in his brain.
'I must cool off' he then declares
And finds the bathroom up the stairs.

Alas, the haven's full of smoke,
And nasty people taking coke.
'Come in,' says Stash, an impish clown
'Come in,' he says, 'and get on down.'

Just then the doorbell trills below,
'Oh no! The pigs! Where can we go?'
'Quick, come with me.' Stash clutches Wayne
Jumps down the pan and pulls the chain.

The Secret Life of Rubber Plants
WAYNE EXPLOITS PIRATE VIDEO

The murky water swills around
Till Wayne and Stash are nearly drowned,
But just in time their cries are heard
By Ploppy Man, a friendly turd

'Wanna have a good time? Then jump on me'
And off they sail, the sights to see.
First on the list's a knocking shop.
He is a lad, our naughty Plop.

'What's going on?' says Stash, all green.
'This is a heavy porno scene.'
'Well shall we stay or shall we go?'
Says Wayne 'Lets make a video.'

The video is really fun
And so they make another one
And then some more and then some shops
And soon they're paying off the cops!

WAYNE GOES ETHNIC

A millionaire at age of six,
Hobnobbing with a bunch of pricks,
But really what's the rat-race worth?
Wayne wants to get back to the earth.
He cracks his pot, puts on his boots
And wanders off to find his roots.

Telling your future by Chinese tea leaves is as easy as telekinesis.

Buy an ordinary packet of China tea and empty it on the floor. Spread the leaves out. Count out one hundred and twenty-three single grains of tea. Count out another one hundred and twenty-three single grains of tea. And another, so the tea is now in many piles of one hundred and twenty-three single grains.

When I last did this, it only took me fourteen hours and you should be able to reach this sort of time with a bit of practice. Once the tea is laid out in piles, take the first three piles and discard the rest.

NOW –

Prepare your question.

Ask the tea leaves your question.

Wait for an hour or so.

Spread the three piles over the rug by rubbing the palm of your hand over them.

Read the tea leaves as follows:

1. *If the first pile is bigger than the second and the third*, this symbolises heaven and earth, conservation and obstruction. The omen portends good and evil and you must not slacken your righteous persistence.

2. *If the second pile is bigger than the first and the third*, this means communion, the mighty ruler declining the great and good approach. It is as though favourable conditions create calculated inaction.

3. *If the third pile is bigger than the first or the second*, this signifies difficulty followed by vigorous returning. Even the ancients abstain from going forth or coming in. It is favourable to have some good fortune!

4. *If two or more piles are the same size*, this signifies hoovering up the tea leaves to get all the bits out of the rug.

The final stage of the Tea Ching is to empty the contents of your hoover into a teapot, add boiling water, and have a nice cup of tea.

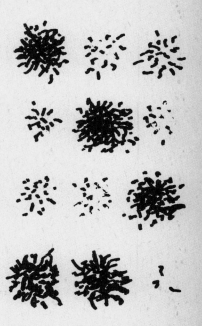

Third Bobo

The Myriad Forms

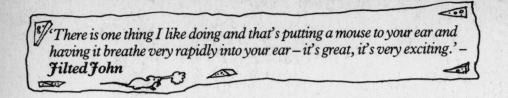

'There is one thing I like doing and that's putting a mouse to your ear and having it breathe very rapidly into your ear – it's great, it's very exciting.' – **Jilted John**

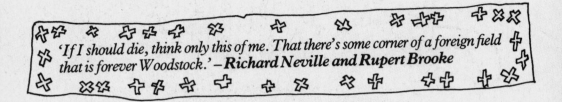

'If I should die, think only this of me. That there's some corner of a foreign field that is forever Woodstock.' – **Richard Neville and Rupert Brooke**

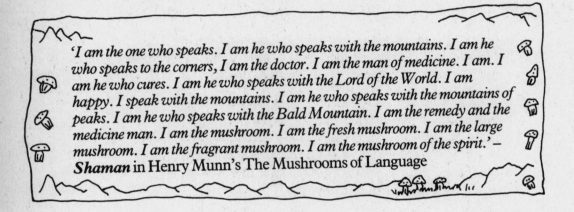

'I am the one who speaks. I am he who speaks with the mountains. I am he who speaks to the corners, I am the doctor. I am the man of medicine. I am. I am he who cures. I am he who speaks with the Lord of the World. I am happy. I speak with the mountains. I am he who speaks with the mountains of peaks. I am he who speaks with the Bald Mountain. I am the remedy and the medicine man. I am the mushroom. I am the fresh mushroom. I am the large mushroom. I am the fragrant mushroom. I am the mushroom of the spirit.' – **Shaman** in Henry Munn's The Mushrooms of Language

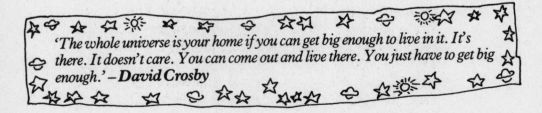

'The whole universe is your home if you can get big enough to live in it. It's there. It doesn't care. You can come out and live there. You just have to get big enough.' – **David Crosby**

The Lords of Existence created everything in the universe from rubber plants to breadheads, from panda bears to doberman pinschers, from one happy lentil to World War III. They seem to be completely impartial.

The Lords of Existence live in a castle somewhere in Scandinavia where they sit at big round-table board meetings just thinking up more things to lay on us mortals.

So they might say, 'Let's send a good vibration down to Kettering.' Or 'Let's cause a five mile tailback between junctions five and six on the M1.' Or 'Let's turn Boy George into a folk hero.' Or 'Let's put a special addictive chemical aura in the Galaxian machines so people like Neil can't get away from amusement arcades.'

They're responsible for every major invention today. They made answerphones to freak you out at home. They made weird organ music to freak you out at the shops. They made special pedestrian crossings that make really unpleasant bleeping noises when you're meant to be crossing the road. They made public telephones where the only number you can dial is the pigs. They made those new public toilets that cost 10p, play Paul McCartney music as you piss and crush you to death if you take too long. They made £1 coins that are trained to vanish and fly back to the Bank of England. They created life in all its myriad forms (you can find them over the page).

Yes, the Lords of Existence made the world into the burnt out urban decay sort of place that it is. And if it's not burnt out, urban and decaying, it's flat, quiet, and boring and raining, like Norfolk.

They really can be total bastards, the Lords of Existence. They were the ones who filled in my scrapbook so there are no more spaces. *And* defaced all the pictures in the *Radio Times* so there's none left for me to do. *And* used all the toilet paper so I have to use a whole two pages of my *Book of the Dead* – and they were the *best two pages*!

We are mere powerless creeps against the power of the fucking Lords of Existence who move in mysterious ways and more often than not go out of their way to make sure I have a really bad time.

I hate you, Lords of Existence. I hate you because you're NEGATIVE, HOSTILE and TOTALLY UNHELPFUL.

I hope you die, okay?

Some of Life's Myriad Forms (and how to fill them in)

ORIENTATION CHECKLIST

Check off each item as it is covered. When orientation is completed, initial and date at the bottom of the checklist.

PRELIMINARY ORIENTATION

_____ "Welcome" section of Handbook
_____ "What's In it for You", "Your New Job Jitters".
_____ Explanation of Orientation and training programme
_____ All Sections and Addendums of the Handbook.

yeah. hamburgers are shit

_NO_ Schedule
_NO_ Call-in Procedure
HEAVY Time Card Procedure
YES Pay Policy
_NO_ Uniforms
_NO_ Parking
YES Breaks & Meals

YEAH Giving Food Away
_____ Honesty & Moral Behaviour
_____ Personal Appearance
_____ Following Directions
_____ The Importance of Questions

I have read and understood all sections and addendums of the Employee Handbook.

Signed _____ *no way*

_____ Orientation film strip no. 1
_____ Completion of paperwork (personnel records, training files, payroll dept etc.) left outstanding
_____ Special store rules, events, and miscellaneous.

_____ Preliminary description of job and overall store functions.
_____ Introduction to Partner name _____ *she's just left*
Tour of store and introduction to crew and management team

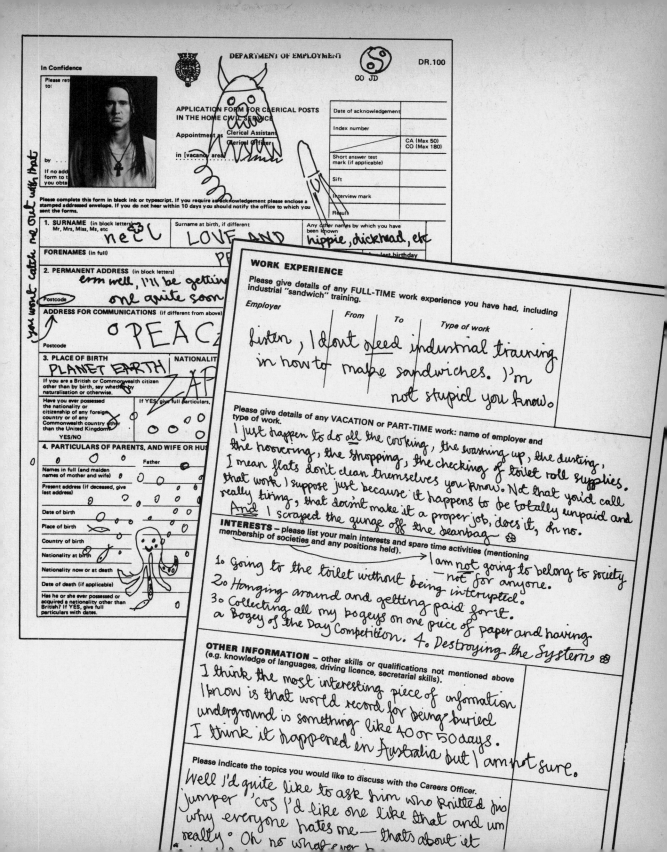

DEPARTMENT OF EMPLOYMENT

In Confidence

DR.100

CO JD

Please ret[urn]
to:

by . . .

If no add[...]
form to t[...]
you obta[...]

APPLICATION FORM FOR CLERICAL POSTS
IN THE HOME CIVIL SERVICE

Appointment as Clerical Assistant
Clerical Officer

in [vacancy area] . . . .

Date of acknowledgement	
Index number	
	CA (Max 50) CO (Max 180)
Short answer test mark (if applicable)	
Sift	
Interview mark	
Result	

Please complete this form in black ink or typescript. If you require an acknowledgement please enclose a stamped addressed envelope. If you do not hear within 10 days you should notify the office to which you sent the forms.

you won't catch me out with that

1. SURNAME (in block letters) Mr, Mrs, Miss, Ms, etc
neil

Surname at birth, if different
LOVE AND

Any other names by which you have been known
hippie, dickhead, etc

FORENAMES (in full)
PE[...]

[...] last birthday

2. PERMANENT ADDRESS (in block letters)
erm well, I'll be gettin[g]
one quite soon

Postcode

ADDRESS FOR COMMUNICATIONS (if different from above)
PEAC[E]

Postcode

3. PLACE OF BIRTH
PLANET EARTH

NATIONALIT[Y]
ZAP

If you are a British or Commonwealth citizen other than by birth, say whether by naturalisation or otherwise.

Have you ever possessed the nationality or citizenship of any foreign country or of any Commonwealth country other than the United Kingdom?
YES/NO

If YES, give full particulars, [...]

4. PARTICULARS OF PARENTS, AND WIFE OR HUS[BAND]

Father

Names in full (and maiden names of mother and wife)

Present address (if deceased, give last address)

Date of birth

Place of birth

Country of birth

Nationality at birth

Nationality now or at death

Date of death (if applicable)

Has he or she ever possessed or acquired a nationality other than British? If YES, give full particulars with dates.

WORK EXPERIENCE

Please give details of any FULL-TIME work experience you have had, including industrial "sandwich" training.

Employer | *From* | *To* | *Type of work*

listen, I dont need industrial training in how to make sandwiches. I'm not stupid you know.

Please give details of any VACATION or PART-TIME work: name of employer and type of work.

I just happen to do all the cooking, the washing up, the dusting, the hoovering, the shopping, the checking of toilet roll supplies. I mean flats don't clean themselves you know. Not that you'd call that work I suppose just because it happens to be totally unpaid and really tiring, that doesn't make it a proper job, does it, oh no. And I scraped the gunge off the beanbag

INTERESTS – please list your main interests and spare time activities (mentioning membership of societies and any positions held).

I am not going to belong to society – not for anyone.

1. Going to the toilet without being interrupted.
2. Hanging around and getting paid for it.
3. Collecting all my bogeys on one piece of paper and having a Bogey of the Day Competition.
4. Destroying the System

OTHER INFORMATION – other skills or qualifications not mentioned above (e.g. knowledge of languages, driving licence, secretarial skills).

I think the most interesting piece of information I know is that world record for being buried underground is something like 40 or 50 days. I think it happened in Australia but I am not sure.

Please indicate the topics you would like to discuss with the Careers Officer.

Well I'd quite like to ask him who knitted his jumper 'cos I'd like one like that and um why everyone hates me — thats about it really. Oh no whatever [...]

On the Astral Plane

The other day I read the weirdest book which totally changed my life. It said that, if you find yourself trapped in the rationalistic straightjacket of the conventional linear time-space continuum of Planet Earth or, in other words, if you're totally bored by reality, there was an alternative apart from falling asleep.

You can depart on a quest for your past lives.

It's easy. Say that, right now, I was feeling really down, depressed and perhaps a bit trapped in the rationalistic straightjacket of the conventional linear time-space continuum. I just lie on the floor, place the palm of my hand in the centre of my forehead, where the Third Eye is (or would be if you could see it) and hit myself approximately once every second...

It's now half an hour later and I think I'm beginning to feel something. Yes, I'm floating upwards, I'm just above the television set. Hey, I'm over the house now, I'm looking down on the street. People are scurrying about like ants, the houses look like matchboxes, and now and then somebody points up to the sky. They're probably saying, 'Oh, there goes Neil, escaping from the linear time-space continuum again in search of his past lives'.

I'm completely alone up here except – who's this? Hey, It's Steve. Hi, Steve, what are you doing up here on the astral plane?

Oh no, that's heavy, man – nobody told me you'd died. What a bummer for Jude.

Anyway, just passing through, okay – I'm on my way to the first century. See you around, Steve. Perhaps.

Now we're travelling back through time, okay, having a really smooth flight, and now we're coming down somewhere. Hey, let's hope I'm a centurian. Or a real druid. Or one of Robin Hood's merry men. Yeah!

Look, there's a lot of people down there on the side of a lake. They're all looking up at me! It's like the Pope flying into Heathrow. Far out!

Now don't panic but I think we're heading for the lake. I really don't like this. I don't know how I'm going to explain when I get back if my hair's all wet. And I'm not even a psychic swimmer.

Oh weird! I'm walking on the water, man. Fucking amazing. Hey look, I'm really freaking them out on the shore. Look, I'll give them a slow love and peace sign. Hey, it's beautiful – they're all on their knees and there has gathered unto me a great multitude who would press upon me to touch my garment.

Did I just say 'garment'? Strange. But I feel really good, you know, but there's something strange going on. What wisdom is this given unto me that mighty works are wrought by my hands?

Oh no, here comes a nutter. He's really shouting at me and everyone's staring as if they expect me to do something really clever. And I've never even seen an unclean spirit before, let alone one who has his dwelling among the tombs, whom no man could bind, no, not with chains.

Right, here goes. Come out of the man, thou unclean spirit, okay?

It worked! I wonder what other great works I could wreak. Why don't I try – oh no, I'm being beamed up, just when I was really getting into that life.

And I'm back in my room. What an incredible past life that was. And I never got the chance to tell myself that in a later life I'd be Neil and it wasn't worth the trip down from the astral plane.

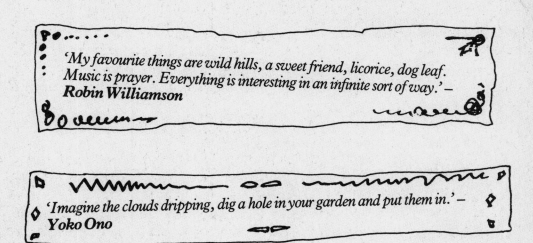

'My favourite things are wild hills, a sweet friend, licorice, dog leaf. Music is prayer. Everything is interesting in an infinite sort of way.' – *Robin Williamson*

'Imagine the clouds dripping, dig a hole in your garden and put them in.' – *Yoko Ono*

ALL THINGS MUST FART

Even while watching Sweeney repeats
Even while lying in new clean sheets
Even while bending for something from the fridge
Even while playing international bridge
Even on the underground even on the bus
Even while searching the mirror for the pus

Buddhist Hindu Christian Pagan
Margaret Thatcher Ronald Reagan
Yellow black pink or brown
In the country in the town
Every peasant every lord
Georgie Best and Anna Ford
All the birdies in the sky
Even Charles and even Di
I wander lonely with my cloud
Sometimes silent sometimes loud
Sometimes rough and sometimes gentle
A whiff of friendship love and lentil

THE NEW WAY OF SEX

A lot of people are really worried about sexual freedom. 'Wow! We've got sexual freedom,' they say. 'What do we do now?'

But today most cool people realise that having a lot of sex and enjoying it is just part of the heavy fascist ritual we're all in on, and anyway it gives you cancer.

They're into a whole new way of sex – it's called the New Way of Sex. Pretty alternative, right? The New Way of Sex doesn't just take place under your duvet with the lights out – it can be happening all the time okay? It's part of life. You might be in a queue at the supermarket, or having a crap, or even just feeling really depressed. The main thing to remember is that, unlike with straight old-fashioned sex, *you don't have to enjoy it*!

In fact, you don't have to be near to or even talk to your partner or partners to have it and you certainly don't have to discuss it afterwards.

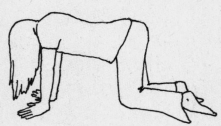

Of course, some people still have difficulty coming to terms with this New Way of Sex. Here are some questions that commonly get asked about it…

1. What are orgasms and where can I get them?

We now know that orgasms were invented by a consortium of drug companies to push the contraceptive pill. It's like a total confidence trick by the straights, like vaginal deodorants and Father Christmas.

2. My partner claims to have had a 'multiple orgasm'. Could I have one of these and would it hurt?

If your partner is 'hooked' on orgasms try to introduce him or her into the New Way of Sex. Like try staring at each other, totally blissed out of your minds, saying 'Oh fucking far out man!' rolling over and falling asleep. If he or she still feels the need to experience so-called 'multiple orgasms', try not to be around when they happen – they can be very negative and really noisy sometimes. I once heard a chick having one in the next door room and it freaked me out for a week.

3. What is 'heavy petting' and is it very expensive?

Well, for a start we don't call them 'pets' these days – that suggests a really straight, animalist attitude towards our fellow creatures. We call them 'animal friends'. So 'heavy petting' is when you develop an irresistible urge for having really heavy animal friends all around you, like a cow in the kitchen, a twenty foot python in the bedroom, a plague of locusts in the toilet. Yeah, this can get very expensive.

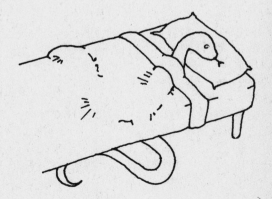

4. People keep asking me why I'm not interested in 'oral sex'. What does this mean?

Like with exams, a lot of people get very nervous about this. They're all right on the straight stuff – the written papers – but, when it comes to the oral, they freak. The thing to remember is like not to panic. Stay relaxed and don't talk too quickly – no one can enjoy orals with a dry mouth. After careful practice, you'll find that you'll be able to get into mutual sessions of oral sex, with first one of you talking and then the other. You may well find that you can sometimes actually talk together at the same time, but this is really stupid because it means you can't hear what the other person is saying.

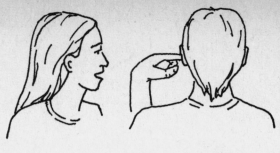

6. A lot of people where I live spend most of their time without any clothes on, touching each other, being beautiful and making squelching noises. But I have never been invited to join in. Is this normal or am I what is called 'a virgin'?

Honestly, all you can think about is rubbing bodies together and wasting Kleenex tissues and making more and more laundry that *someone* has got to go and do, right? I mean, the whole thing is getting stupid. I think they're all having a really boring time in there anyway. They're all stupid. I hate them.

5. Are there any new and unusual positions I could try with my partner that might enhance our sexual enjoyment?

Look, I've already told you that you don't have to enjoy it, right? In fact, some of the best of the New Way of Sex can be really horrible. God, you're stupid. Anyway, once you've understood that, there's hundreds of new positions to try out. What about some unexpected places like telephone kiosks, revolving doors, in the fridge, station platforms, motorway cafes, in a dustcart. Or have you thought of being in different rooms, or different towns, or even different realities?

SKY SHOW

Sky Show

Starring the end of the day

Co-starring the beginning of the night

Sky Show 2

Starring the beginning of the night

Co-starring the end of the day

The New Urban Celtic Pagan Awareness

In celtic times, before bad vibes had even been invented, everyone was really together and natural.

One of the secrets why they were all so totally loving and unhostile was that they were heavily into what they called Total Celtic Pagan Awareness Workshops.

What they used to do was find something really organic which had special powers, like an oak or an ash or a ferret, and worship it as a great symbol of natures way.

These days, now that we're all trapped in the concrete nightmare of Planet Earth's total urban decay, finding, oaks, ashes or ferret trees near where you live is not as easy as it once was. That's why the New Urban Celtic Pagan Movement was set up - to help us all find new, relevant twentieth century symbols of natures way.

Now they've discovered that the most important symbol of natures way that can be found in an urban situation. It is the rare and sacred white turd.

Where do white turds come from? No one ever sees them as they arrive on this earth. Who leaves them? Racist police dogs? Animal friends who have been given Barium meals? The milky Bar kid? Of course not—everyone knows that's totally unscientific and really stupid.

No white turds are left by faries. Remember The ancient rhyme:

" Around y playgrounde, fayries flitte,
Yn oakes y playe and yn white shitte."

So, ever since I became celtically aware, I've started searching for white turds wherever I go. I collect them, lay them out in special places around the house. By my bed. Hanging from pieces of string on the wall. In a magic turd ring at the top of the stairs.

Or sometimes I just leave them in people's pockets as a secret good luck token.

Lets dance around our magic turds
And sing these happy little words.

A world of tiny happy things
Are with us in our turdy rings.

The pretty flies, the host of germs,
Lovely, wriggly little worms.

I'll touch you turdy, every day,
The Urban Celtic Pagan Way.

So sing these happy, little words

And dance around the magic turds.

WHY THE AYATOLLAH WAS RIGHT

You know those people who go away and you don't see them for a while and suddenly they're back, wearing sun-glasses and saying things like, 'Wow man I've just been to L.A. man and I looked in on the Big Apple on the way back I was really hanging loose man and I was you know driving down the freeway? And you know doing Death Row in a Pontiac? Like way out babe Stateside's where it's at man. I'm gonna go straight back there as soon as I can because England's like so uncool these days you know?'

And all you want to say to them is, 'Well, why don't you fuck off back there right now and stop bringing us down even more?'

Because the fact is that Stateside, America, the US of A or whatever you like to call it really isn't that cool at all.

I mean, Kennedy was KILLED, right? Martin Luther King was KILLED.

And the Incredible String Band were shouted off stage on their FIRST GIG over there. In fact, that's why it's called 'over there' – because it's OVER, it's the END as far as Stateside's concerned, and not just for the Incredibles – for everyone.

Most of it comes down to bread which is really typical. The Americans invented money and now they've organized it so that, whatever happens, all the money in the world will eventually end up there.

And I can prove this is true, right? Have you ever watched *Dallas*? (Of course, they wouldn't put on a show called *Ipswich* or *Leeds*, would they?) Well, I never watch it but, if you saw that episode where the guy who lives in the skyscraper with the oil derrick in his backyard had to hassle everyone for bread so that he could have a really big barbecue around a swimming pool to show off his enormous new car to his girlfriend to persuade her to have a face-lift because his wife caught herpes in the last episode – if you saw all that, you'll know that in every five minutes of *Dallas*, you see enough money to support at least three struggling South American republics. Which just proves that these days any serious money in the world just has to end up Stateside.

Soon the only money you'll be allowed will be dollars. You'll have to pay busfares with them and the bus might take you to the shops via Philadelphia. Or you might have to go to New Mexico to get change for the launderette.

There is one good thing, I suppose. At least they have some good whole food restaurants in San Francisco and they're all really into lentils. I had a friend who went there who said you can get psychedelic muesli and wheatgerm milkshakes in one hundred and one natural flavours from this amazing shop run by totally self-sufficient Red Indians with solar panels.

And I suppose the Grateful Dead and the Doors came from America. And so did the sixties. And the Red Indians. And if you book a ticket for the space shuttle and there's no seats left on it, they run a special stand-by service. That's quite nice of them, really. And their telephones always work. And they always say 'You're welcome' if you say 'Thank you'. And the waitresses say things like, 'Hi, I'm Charlene, I'm your waitress for the day, are you ready to order?'

And California Red comes from America.

And they're always sending things over like Macdonalds to help us eat faster and *The Texas Chainsaw Massacre* to help us throw it up again and now we've got skateboards and *Starsky and Hutch* and AIDS and cruise missiles and Coca Cola and cocaine and Paul Gambaccini and *Time* magazine and superbitches and the American Way.

Hey, maybe we're in America already. Far out, man!

Have a nice day.

'If you really want to travel, why can't you just transfer yourself — by changing your matter into energy and back again. Why can't you? What's stopping you from doing it? The answer is in your head.'
IT

A lot of people think that dreams are boring and not worth discussing. But it has now been scientifically proved that they are incredibly important really and not boring at all because they reveal our character, our past, our future, and sometimes our friends' future, if we really know how to interpret them. In fact, the most boring dream you ever had will have more meaning than the most significant event in your so-called waking reality.

There are about one thousand theories about dreams, why we have them, what they mean, how long they last, whether we can have them when we are awake, what is illusion and what is fantasy, is life but a waking dream and so on. Some of these are a bit complicated and not very interesting, okay, but the subject is so important and I've read so many really freaky *Test Your Own Dream Power* books that I think I should go through them one by one. So, like, get your cup of tea now, okay?

The first one is that dreamland, the so-called Land of Nod, is in fact more real than the world we think is real because the one that's really real we always forget about as soon as we get out of bed so that it seems less real to us than the real one. But this Land of Nod is a special, magic realm where all the little everyday things we tend to take for granted become incredibly important for reasons we can never quite understand.

This brings me back to the question on which this second theory rests. In fact, some people think it's the question on which the whole of life rests. It's the heaviest question you could ever be asked, heavier than anything that's ever been on *Mastermind*. It is:

WHAT IS REALITY?

I don't know.

The second theory about dreams is not quite as interesting as the first one. In fact, it's probably the most uninteresting one there is, apart from the six hundred and fifty seventh, which we'll be coming to a bit later.

Are you ready for this? The sort of dreams you have depends on what you have just had to eat, or what you've had during the day if you happen not to have been to the toilet before you went to bed. So if you've eaten a really heavy hamburger, full of additives and sugar and salt and carbohydrates and colouring and blood and insecticides and nuclear waste and meat, you'll almost definitely dream about being a cowboy, surrounded by nuclear power plants, and you'll be shooting at everything. And every time the burger turns a corner in your intestine the dream will get more violent until the whole Mexican army, who have really bad teeth and don't look very well, gun you down like at the end of *Bonnie and Clyde,* except it's not blood that comes out of the bullet holes but little worms of meat, like a Big Mac being pushed through a mincer.

On the other hand, if you've just eaten a wholesome, satisfying, totally alternative plate of kidney beans, you'll most likely dream about running through the woods with sitar music playing. Or if the beans weren't soaked properly, you'll probably find that the meadow is a bit marshy in places and, if you've been really greedy, it will turn into a steaming, smelly quicksand that swallows you up.

This theory shows how important it is for you to avoid constipation. Imagine what all those dreams piling up inside of you could do to the karma of your dreamworld. You could start getting really weird dreams about meat oozing out of quicksands, or cowboys playing the sitar.

So you could say that when you go to the toilet you're just getting rid of all your used dreams. Maybe that's why it's such a good place for writing songs! Hey!

I sometimes wonder what sort of dream you'd have if you'd swallowed three packets of bubble-gum? Or a lump of coal? Or a very long shopping-list? That would be a pretty boring dream, I suppose. Not that being boring makes it less important. This theory's quite a boring theory but it's probably true. Sometimes the truth is boring. Right? In my life, the truth is almost always boring. In fact, probably the more boring things are the truer they are and ZZZZZZZZZZZZZZZZZZZZZZZZZZZZZZZZZZZZZZZZZZZZZZZZZZZZZZZZZZZZZZ

Oh no it's Frank Sinatra's Christmas Special!

And yes here he is ladies and gentlemen my old buddy and special guest tonight. — it's **Neil!**

Whatever you do don't call him Godfather.

Hey Neil, shake that asbestos dust off your shoulders and come on in, Gee I havent seen you since ooo, way back. When was that rehearsal Neil? No seriously what are you going to sing for us to put us in a Christmas mood?

D'you know 'The Streets of London'?

This is the worst thing that's ever happened to me

No I dont know that one Neil. Hey. Youre not telling the Folks back home that you've come on our little ole Christmas Special without a Yuletide song to sing. Hows that, ladies & gentlemen?

Let me take you by the hand···

She drinks methylated spirits from an old cider bottle that's why the Lady is a tramp!

Plink Plunk

Now your starter for a Krypton factor of 18, what are the names of 4 of the 5 Nolan Sisters? take your time and it's goodbye to your tongue if you get it wrong.

Ohhh WWooo WWWW

'Most westerners find it difficult to attain unity with the source of light in the same way that most easterners find it hard to get hold of reasonable hi-fi equipment.' – **Timothy Leary**

'The circle of this world is like a ring:
There is no doubt at all that we are the
Naqsh, the Design of its bezel.'
Idries Shah, The Way of the Sufi

'You don't feel like some big rock star when you've got your head stuck down the toilet.' – **Johnny Winter**

'There are forty people in the world and five of them are hamburgers.' – **Captain Beefheart**

'Pop is the perfect religious vehicle: it's as if God had come down to earth and seen all the ugliness that was being created and had chosen pop to be the great force for love and beauty.' – **Donovan**

GARDENING SECTION

Well, for a start gardening has got nothing to do with looking after the bit of mud and grass and trees outside your back door. That's just such a narrow view of what a garden is. So you can just forget it.

And it's got nothing to do with those shops where you can get green plastic fencing and peat and flowers and plants and growbags and things, although I quite like the little concrete gnomes.

The worst experience I ever had at a so-called 'gardening shop' was when I once bought a growbag. I took it home and watered it for like months but nothing grew out of it. Nothing at all. Someone told me that you had to plant something in it but that was stupid – if you have to go to all that hassle, why bother to get a growbag in the first place?

I decided it was a rip-off until one day I looked at it and realised that, although nothing had grown in it, the bag itself was ever so slightly bigger than it had been. And I thought, 'So *that's* what they mean by a growbag!'

I stopped watering it at once. I mean, I didn't like the idea of killing a living thing but who knows how big it could have grown? I think that's really dangerous – they should put a warning on the side of the packet:
A GROWBAG IS FOR LIFE NOT JUST FOR CHRISTMAS.

Oh no, I just thought! What if it gets really angry that I haven't watered it for ages and decides to eat me instead? What if it's a killer growbag? There might be killer growbags everywhere. Watch out for killer growbags, everybody. Just when you thought it was safe to go back in the greenhouse! The Growbags That Ate Paris! Invasion of the Growbags!

I bet the guy who invented growbags feels really guilty now. Maybe he's had to get himself a new identity so that he can live with himself and the ugly, evil thing that he created. The growbags that turned out to be far bigger and more powerful than man's ability to control them. The Growbag Syndrome. Hey, maybe someone should make a film about it before it's all too late and get Jane Fonda to be in it, and Felicity Kendal could get a load of people together to do a benefit for it. GROWBAGS AT DRURY LANE. But, even then, it might be too late.

Well, that's definitely the last time I visit a garden shop for anything. No, there's more to a garden than that.

Because a garden can be anywhere. In your mind. In the fridge. In your shoe. In fact, the whole idea of having a 'gardening section' is totally straight and stupid because, if you have your head together, life is a garden. This whole Book of the Dead could just be a lovely little rock garden, with coloured stones and pixies with fishing rods and psychedelic kingfishers freaking out among the marigolds.

So here are a few things that the true gardener can do:

Look at the garden under your fingernail, replenish it with the lush, rich soil you can scrape from behind your ear

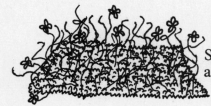

Search for hairs on the floor behind the toilet and plant a forest in a friend's flannel

Skip through the orchard of a relationship in search of the bright, elusive butterfly of breakfast

Look under your mattress, marvel at the myriad allness of the smallness of the mould growing there

Draw the fresh running water of illusion from the windmills of your headache

Knock down the walls of your perception and plant some lovely rambling notions there

PHILOSOPHY II
Marcuse: myth or mind-trip?

So this is the only essay I'm going to do this year, right? And I'm only doing it because everyone else seems to have a philosophy and I don't see why I shouldn't have one.

What is philosophy? Can philosophy exist when you're not actually thinking about it? Do dandelions have a sense of their own being? And what about dolphins? Oh, wow, what a freaky thought! Perhaps somewhere there's a dolphin writing a really heavy essay on dolphin philosophy right now. Weird.

Well, one thing's for sure – philosophy isn't about heavy, heavy books with long paragraphs and no pictures.

Because the more you read, the more you realize that long words and ideas and books are just totally irrelevant when it comes to philosophy. I can learn more about truth from a beautiful chance encounter or a Mary Hopkin song than from Marshall Marcuse and his so-called massaging mediums. He's just not relevant and I don't want to discuss him, okay?

Hey, just look at a leaf, really study it carefully – if possible when you're totally out of it.

Suddenly you can see the truth.

The truth is the leaf.

The leaf is the truth.

Truth leaf.

Leaf truth.

Oh God, it's so fucking beautiful, man!

Too short —

Neil

PHILOSOPHY II (for the last time, okay?)
Aristotle: an existentialist before his time?

I really don't see why I keep having to do essays when everyone knows that philosophy is about *feeling* not *doing*. Nobody's explained why I can't just stay at home and *feel* Aristotle, instead of doing all this writing which makes my brain hurt. This really is pointless, but here goes.

Aristotle was *not* an existentialist before his time, okay? Everyone knows that he was the fascist who lived on the island of Catharsis until he blew it when he started getting it together with Kennedy's wife. It's obvious he couldn't even have heard of Jean-Paul Sartre and the other boulevardier philosophers because Paris is miles away from Catharsis and they didn't have telephones in those days and didn't speak the same language.

Since this is the last essay I'm ever going to do, I'm going to write about my own subject, all right. It is: WHY THE HUNCHBACK OF NOSTRADAMUS WAS THE MOST IMPORTANT PHILOSOPHER OF ALL TIME.

Some people have been quite surprised to hear that the Hunchback of Nostradamus is the most important philosopher of all time. That's because they never read the books I've read about him and they don't know his incredible secret, and they just want to say anything to put him down anyway.

The truth is that he wasn't just an evil-looking deviant zombie with a lopsided face who could only speak French. In fact, he was a really good guy and, as anyone who has seen the film will tell you, he spoke English perfectly well unlike the rest of fourteenth century Paris who spoke with dubbed American accents.

But, apart from that, he had this amazing secret life. Every night, after a hard day swinging on bells or shooting his film, he'd come back home and work on his great project – predicting the whole of world history to the end of time. Incredible, right?

Now this is really interesting because, like all other really important people, he was never taken seriously by *anyone*. Members of the French court would lay all sorts of shit on him saying 'Yes, but how d'you know there will be a fearful conflagration between 1914 and 1918?' He'd shrug and say 'I just got a hunch that's all.' That was his joke.

Well, at least he had a joke, unlike Aristotle.

Recently people have started realizing how accurate the Hunchback's predictions are. In fact, Hitler used the *Prophecies* to map out the whole of World War II and, if he hadn't had a copy with some pages stuck together, the whole course of the war might have been totally different.

I could write for pages about the many triumphs of the Hunchback of Nostradamus, but why should I? I'm not going to pass this exam anyway. So I'll jump straight to the important bit. Why is the Hunchback of Nostradamus so much more important than any other philosopher?

Put it this way, okay? Would you be more interested in someone who told you that any significant truth which is comparable to a generalization must by its nature be self-confirming or in someone who could tell you exactly what was going to happen to you?
Enough said.

Neil

PS For instance, I know what you're going to say at the end of this – you're going to say 'See me', aren't you?

see me

Fourth Bobo

The Acid Flower

HERE IS ELF!

ELF is like my own alternative magazine. Well actually it *is* my own alternative magazine.

You can cut ELF out from Neil's *Book of the Dead* and carry it away with you as a magic paper token. Otherwise you could just read it.

ELF has all sort of alternative magazine type things in it – reviews, raps, reports, messages and LOVE.

You will also find some nice words and pictures from other, antique magazines as you read ELF. They are to help remind you of a time when love and awareness were everywhere – a time before the Breadhead Conspiracy (see this issue of ELF) came along and infiltrated the elfin world.

By the way, if you do cut out ELF and give it to aware strangers you meet upon the highway, be sure to give it with love and not charge more than the equivalent value of fourteen pages of this book. Anything more means that you're making a profit out of *Neil's Book of the Dead* which, rightfully speaking, should come to me. On the other hand, if you manage to hit them for something really heavy like £1.50, we could go 50/50 if you agreed to buy another book for me to replace the one you vandalized because, I mean, it was quite hard making ELF and it took a really long time and anyway what about VAT? That's 15 per cent on £1.50 – that's 22½p, right? And I get to keep the odd ½p. okay?

ELF – THE WONDROUS NEWS FOR ELFIN PEOPLE .....

Beyond the brain and the totally blown mind lies....

ELF

Peace, Stranger . . . . You are now entering the magical world of ELF.

ELF is an offering from a really beautiful mind that believes that no magazine, not even *Time Out* or *NME*, is giving us REAL NEWS.

Because REAL NEWS is not about voting and the bomb and who's died on *Coronation Street*. It's not about action, events, things and other non-elfin concepts – it's about INACTION and VERY NICE THOUGHTS. REAL NEWS is happening all around us all the time – in our minds, in an acorn or on the wings of the tiniest wasp.

As you read these pages, you may feel the hand of friendship and love reaching out between the words. It wants to touch you, to share your humanity. It wants to talk elfin with you for a while. It wants to know if you paid for this magazine because, if you just 'borrowed' it from a fellow elf, then that's really negative because the ELFIN DIGGER is bringing you all this love totally at his own expense.

Reach out for the hand. Touch it. Hold it. Put £1.50 in it.

Breathe, smile, love – for there be ELFIN PEOPLE about!

Elfin Digger

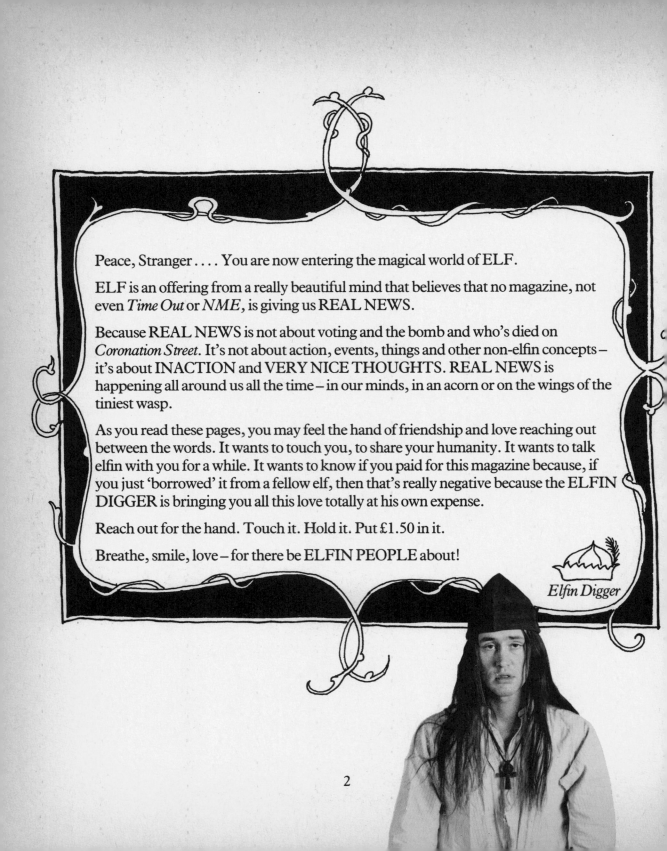

Within Elfin Wood

THE BREADHEAD CONSPIRACY

Have you ever wondered what life's heaviest bummers have in common?

Like why there are fewer and fewer black fruit gums every year and more and more horrid orange ones?

Or why policemen walk differently from anyone else?

Or why Paul McCartney's next collaboration is going to be with Kenny Lynch?

Or why they killed off like *everyone* at the end of *Blake's Seven*?

Or why, when you get crossed lines, it's always the same two women talking about someone who's in hospital?

Or why party political broadcasts are *always* on every channel at the same time?

Or why budgerigar bells are no longer sold in head shops any more?

Or why people suddenly stopped laughing at Elton John and started taking him seriously?

Or why George Harrison has got a jacuzzi?

Or why no one ever *ever* mentions any of these things?

The answer is one of the heaviest trips you can imagine.

It's called – the Breadhead Conspiracy.

What is the Conspiracy? Where did it start? Who's in it? And what can we do about it?

Dire straights (and I don't mean the band, okay?)

When the astronauts landed ten thousand years ago, they immediately started undermining the alternative, ecologically sound and totally peaceful lifestyle of Planet Earth by sending in some really dire straights to move among the people.

As time went on, the straights reached positions of power all over the world and started behaving really negatively. Among the sons and daughters of alien astronauts were Attila the Hun, Henry VIII, Boadicea, Colonel Custer, Margaret Thatcher and Abba.

Yet, until about fifteen years ago, Planet Earth contained a balance of real human beings and straights. That is, until the Breadhead Conspiracy was hatched.

It was a time when the real human beings – or 'heads' as they had become known – were celebrating the dawning of the Age of Aquarius. They could do anything then: write the best music in the history of the world, have the heaviest religious experiences, and bigger orgasms than anyone had ever had before.

The dire straights were worried. They had thought *they* now had the power. They had untold wealth. They led every country in the world, except Canada. Yet something was going wrong. No one was listening to them any more.

Richard Branson

So they infiltrated the ranks of the heads and the Age of Aquarius soon became the Age of the Breadhead. The very same heads who, a few solstices ago, were getting into peace and friendship now started getting into fast sports cars with blonde breadhead chicks.

Gradually they forgot that they had ever been heads. Their whole behaviour changed. They imported frisbees. They opened antique emporiums. They ripped off groups. They set up chains of discount record shops and hairdressers. They discovered computers and programmed them to write hit tunes. They opened antique emporiums. They snorted cocaine and listened to Richard Pryor tapes. Together they changed the beautiful elfin society of the Age of Aquarius into the polluted breadhead swamp that it is today.

So, elfin folk, don't smile at the breadheads. They are out to destroy.

5

THE BREADHEAD CONSPIRACY

This page shows how they looked when they were human beings (*left*) and how the same people look now, staring through the prison bars of their little breadhead brains (*right*).

But these are just a few of them. Remember – breadheads are *everywhere*.

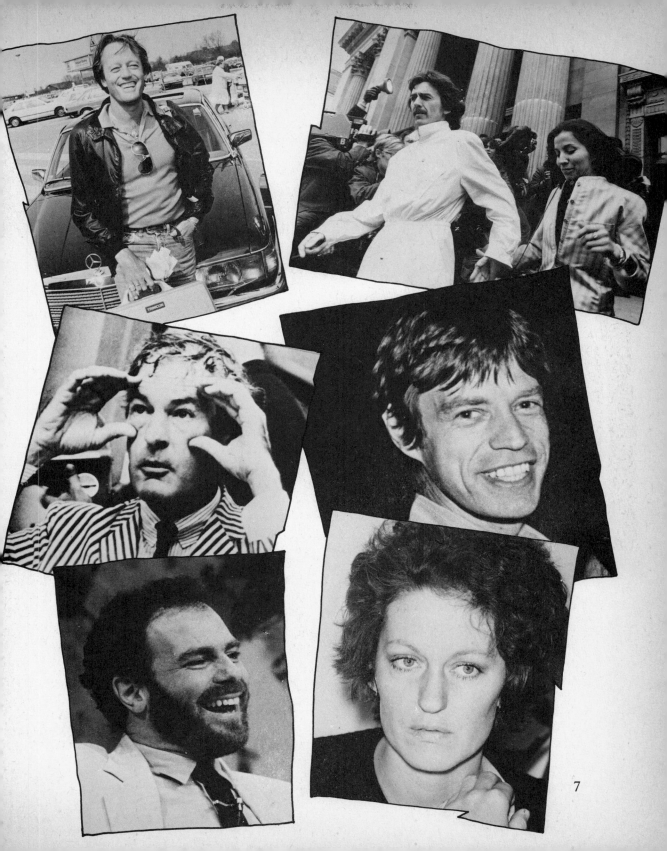

7

An exclusive ELF interview

THE ELFIN DIGGER
RAPS WITH NEIL

*Neil is one busy elf these days. He has
starred on television. He did the famous
Lentil Tour. He has turned down big parts
in several commercials and is rumoured to be
working on a major concept involving
washing up through psychokinetic
paratechnology. Not bad for the guy the
Financial Times once described as
'essentially very boring'.*

*I caught up with Neil in front of his mirror
where he was pulling the hair out of his left
nostril.*

8

Neil: Hi, Neil!

Neil: Wha-What? Who are you? What are you doing in my mirror?

Neil: I'm the Elfin Digger – you can call me Neil, Neil – I'm doing an exclusive rap with you for the pages of ELF magazine.

Neil: Is that the magazine for those who brim with cosmic elfin awareness?

Neil: That's the one.

Neil: Great. Okay, let's rap, Neil.

Neil: Well, I guess we know about Neil the legend. You're a busy elf these days. You've starred on television. You've done the famous Lentil Tour. You've turned down –

Neil: Hey, I'm sorry to interrupt, Neil, but didn't you say all this at the top of the page?

Neil: Look, Neil, let me do this my way, okay? I'm just like getting into this, right? Yeah, now I was aware of the whole Neil phenomenom from a very early age. I remember some of your very first toilet experiences, your schooldays and that close friendship with little Rupert Thompson and how the teachers had to separate you in classes, and then your very first wet dream and how you thought it was –

Neil: Hey, come on, Neil, do we have to go into all this?

Neil: I thought it would be interesting if I painted a word picture of the human side of a living legend.

Neil: And don't fucking patronize me, okay? I really don't like the way you're doing this interview.

Neil: D'you think one of the reasons why you're so shy of the media is that basically, because of your big success and all that money, you're totally out of touch with the real world?

Neil: No that's not true – I never saw any of the money –

NEIL: MMM, THIS SPAGHETTI'S DELICIOUS . . .

Neil: Yes well frankly, I don't think that's going to have any credibility with the kids. I mean, where's the relevance for them in what you're doing now?

NEIL: HEY, NEIL, COULD WE JUST ORDER ANOTHER ROUND OF DACQUIRIS BEFORE YOU GO ON?

Neil: It's dub not dacquiris I think we should be talking about –

Neil: I'm really not happy about the way this is going, right? When I had this idea of rapping with myself to fill up a few columns of ELF, I had no idea it was going to be so heavy. I was promised this was going to be a soft interview.

NEIL: HEY, WHERE DID YOU GET THAT SHIRT, NEIL? I'VE JUST GOT TO ORDER SIX OF THOSE BEFORE I FLY BACK?

Neil: All right. Let me put it another way. The word on the streets is that Neil has sold out, that the Neil who had something valid to say has been taken over by a media Neil, a Neil that likes green cocktails and wears Ted Lapidus shirts.

NEIL: HEY, IS IT TRUE THAT BILLY AND PAMELA LIVE ROUND HERE? I'D JUST LOVE TO CALL IN ON BILLY AND PAMELA!

Neil: No, that's totally untrue what you're saying and now I'm going to finish pulling the hair out of my nostrils. This was a really bad idea –

Neil: So you would admit then that, while you're happy to knock others publicly, when it comes to yourself, you're not –

NEIL: WHERE IS THAT DACQUIRI? YOU KNOW, I'M NOT

USED TO WAITING FOR MY DRINKS?

Neil: Look, I'm really sorry about this hassle. I didn't know it was going to be like this—

Neil: So you're just not prepared to lay yourself open to public scrutiny for fear of exposure as just another typical hyped-up media wanker, leeching off the kids who put you—

NEIL: HEY LISTEN, NEIL, YOU DON'T NEED THIS. YOU SHOULDN'T HAVE TO INTERVIEW YOURSELF. DOES WARREN INTERVIEW HIMSELF? JUST GET YOUR PRESS OFFICE TO CALL UP *TIME* MAGAZINE FOR A FEATURE.

Neil: I find this very significant—

NEIL: AND FOR CHRIST'S SAKE CHASE UP THAT DACQUIRI FOR ME! WHERE *IS* THAT MAITRE D'?

Neil: Was that Warren Beatty you were talking about? You know Warren Beatty?

NEIL: SURE I KNOW WARREN. CRAZY TIMES, CRAZY TIMES . . .

Neil: Would you like to tell the readers of ELF about your crazy times with Warren Beatty, Neil?

NEIL: HEY, OUT WEST WE HAVE AN OLD SAYING WHICH GOES, 'DON'T SHIT IN YOUR OWN JACUZZI'. THAT MEANS I'M NOT TELLING YOU SHIT ABOUT MY OLD PAL WARREN.

Neil: Hey, guys, I think we've filled up enough space now, okay. Can I get on with my nostrils now?

In the next issue of ELF: Neil and Nastassia Kinski—the untold story.

The most beau tiful person of all time

Who wrote:

'Oh dear. Smile at several people today. You may save a life'?

Here are some clues. These days, he writes for *The Times*. He also does quite a lot of voice-overs for telly adverts.

No idea? What if I tell you that he sometimes appears on the special geriatrics edition of *Top of the Pops,* trying to look bored when it's clear to everyone he just loves bopping around to the music of Fun Boy Three with the out-of-work actors that make up the audience.

Yes, of course, it's John Peel.

It's an incredible fact that this old man was once the most incredibly beautiful person of all time.

Here are some sweet flowers from the very nice 'Perfumed Garden' magazine columns he used to write.

'It would be nice to live in a painting. I think I would live in Paul Klee's 'Landscape with Yellow Birds' – there is plenty of room for you there.'

'John Peel sends his vibrations with sorrow for silence in this and last issue of IT. Sends message that personal hang-ups are disturbing his time-space arrangements. Forgive him. He still loves.'

'The sky is overcast but the clouds are leaving my thoughts. Let us exchange sunshine soon. It is good to be part of you.'

'Walk far from the towns, touch the bark of a thousand trees, shoeless. There are a million flowers which have grown just for you, please go and find them and let them know your peace.'

There are sparrows and fountains and roses in my head. I think I'll go for a walk and then bring these silly words to you. Sometimes I don't have enough time to think of loving you – that is very wrong.

'You are the only hope I have. Kiss me this summer.'

'Have an understanding and elevated holiday and accept my love, wrapped and placed softly beneath your tree.'

'When you're feeling very young go to the children's playground in the Bayswater Road corner of Kensington Gardens and sit and stare at the elves on the tree there. Then go among the peacocks in Holland Park and find some of your own.'

11

When girls were still chicks

There was a magical time before chicks started getting into independence, running the country and having their own orgasms. During the Age of Aquarius, they'd be happy just hanging around and grooving and bringing sunshine to the guys.

'Some organized suggestions for (Dutch) Provo sexual reform from our fantasy department...A White Woman Plan to parallel the White Bike Plan might be useful – that is, there was a time when a bike painted white was common property to any Provo.'
IT

'During mass confrontations, girls are everywhere – at sit-ins, be-ins, loot-ins..."Chicks up front" is a constant battle cry.'
Richard Neville, Playpower

'An earth-aim of mine is to hold my arm up until I am admired by nine hundred million girls.'
Bruce, OZ

'Dr G, the groupie jumps up to get ready to go to the Macrobiotic (because she likes it!) and rattles on while she fluffs out her hair about the necessity of being into your own thing, of getting back into your body so if you understand and admire an artist your nipples erect when you read a line of him or hear a bar of his music (like berries under the brown gauze of her long dress whipped with old lace) so Norman Mailer's penis blossoms in her head, stopping suddenly to swoop and kiss me on the mouth with her hand cupping my breast as naturally as when we shall come to life among the flowers of Beulah.'
Germaine Greer

12

'Suck, don't bite.'
Danae, Friends

'Crabs are beautiful.'
Donovan

'One way to a girl's mind is through her cunt.'
Richard Neville, Playpower

'I think every girl should be a plaster caster – try it at least once. It's going to be a significant element in the revolution.'
Cynthia Plaster Caster of the Plaster Casters of Chicago

'The IT-Girl Maureen wears a transparent dress designed by two local tripped-out chicks, Karen and Angela. Light does fantastic things with it. It is the new trip sensuality. Buy one for your psychedelic mistress.'
By the IT-Girl's green candle

An interview with Peter Fonda

All right, so this first appeared in *Rolling Stone* in 1971. That doesn't mean it's not really relevant today. Anyway, he was talking about his new film *Deleted Portions of the Zapruder Film.*

'There's a guy in a window with four chicks. It's like opening a closet door and seeing rats, only you don't really see them. And the camera gets up and each time they're doing something new. He's got a bow, or a gun, or a knife. And they're nude or in garter belts.

And there's this long-haired Oriental biker holding an AR-15, like the guy did in the Dallas jail.

And there's a big cardboard cut-out of me draped in a flag. And it falls forward, falls forward.

And two stills of the Pope's assassination.

Life's photos of My Lai.

And it all builds up. The guy with the chicks finally pees out of the window. A chick inserts a dildo.

The camera pulls back from the falling cardboard statue and there I am with a gun.

It's about eight minutes long.'

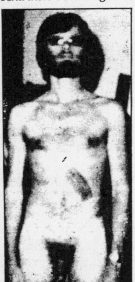

AN ELFIN POEM FROM ORACLE MAGAZINE....

'simply
sit
        undisturbing   **THE**
                                      PEACE
LETTING it   flow
(as they put it)

LEAF TALK....

'Why not use a LEAF as our SYMBOL of COMMUNICATION? Supposing you see someone you like the look of, male or female, go over and hand them a leaf. Just an ordinary fallen leaf from a tree ... A simple tree leaf will not be missed by anyone and may mean the first human contact in a long, grey day, week or month even, to the one who receives it ...

So if you see anyone you would like to talk to, walk over and silently hand them a leaf. Then wait expectantly ... Don't be put off by uptight chicks or incomprehending males. Keep on trying until CONVERSATION LEAVES become a natural part of this generation's *Ritual Consciousness. Gandalf's Garden Issue No. 5*

The Walrus Speaks

'It's difficult when you've learned that everything is just the act and everything is beautiful or ugly, or you like it or you don't, things are backward or they're forward. And dogs are less intelligent than humans and suddenly you realize that whilst all of that is right, it's all wrong as well. Dogs aren't less intelligent to dogs, and the ashtray's happy to be an ashtray and the hang-up still occurs.'

'Starvation in India doesn't worry me one bit. Not one iota, it doesn't, man.

'At the back of my brain somewhere is there is something telling me now that everything is beautiful...It tells me that everything is beautiful and everything is great and fine and that instead of imposing things like "Oh, I don't like that television show", or "No, I don't like the theatre", "No, no, I don't like so and so", that I know really that it's all great, and that everything's great and that there's no bad ever, if I can think of it all as great.'

Gifts from our Elfin Mailbag

'Dear Sir
I saw my first flower girl the other day and I was dismayed to think that she could go about town with an escort of long-haired youths. What a sight for we older folk! And to think that budgies are being deprived of bells for their cages because there is a run on pet shops for the little bells that give our feathered friends endless joy.
Yours,
Mrs Gillian Hush, letter to the Daily Mail

'Dear OZ
Pure & eurythmic, clear & polymorphic. I wonder if anyone realizes exactly how content a glass of water must be.
Paul, Frank and Zettusa, letter to OZ

Dear ELF
I am totally disappointed with the latest issue of ELF. Could you get your elfin brain together and answer me this:
    What's with the fucking sixties? This is 1984, right? If I hear the names of Frank Zappa, Stevie Winwood, Emma Peel or any other of those geriatrics again, I'm going to spew – all over ELF.
    What kind of shit *is* this love, peace and understanding? D'you really think the kids today have time for that kind of nostalgia trip?
    Don't you understand, Elfin Digger – THE TIMES THEY ARE A-CHANGIN'!!! I'm going to stuff ELF down the toilet.
neil

I think that's a really negative attitude and I hope the Breadhead Conspiracy gets you, if they haven't already. Doing this magazine was the worst idea I ever had – I'm never ever going to do another one.
Elfin Digger.

15

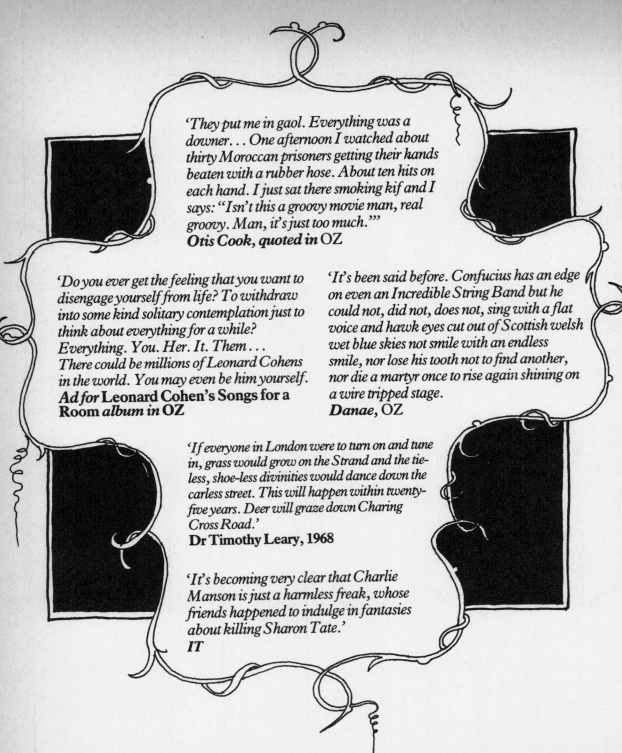

'They put me in gaol. Everything was a downer... One afternoon I watched about thirty Moroccan prisoners getting their hands beaten with a rubber hose. About ten hits on each hand. I just sat there smoking kif and I says: "Isn't this a groovy movie man, real groovy. Man, it's just too much."'
Otis Cook, quoted in OZ

'Do you ever get the feeling that you want to disengage yourself from life? To withdraw into some kind solitary contemplation just to think about everything for a while? Everything. You. Her. It. Them... There could be millions of Leonard Cohens in the world. You may even be him yourself.
Ad for Leonard Cohen's Songs for a Room album in OZ

'It's been said before. Confucius has an edge on even an Incredible String Band but he could not, did not, does not, sing with a flat voice and hawk eyes cut out of Scottish welsh wet blue skies not smile with an endless smile, nor lose his tooth not to find another, nor die a martyr once to rise again shining on a wire tripped stage.
Danae, OZ

'If everyone in London were to turn on and tune in, grass would grow on the Strand and the tie-less, shoe-less divinities would dance down the carless street. This will happen within twenty-five years. Deer will graze down Charing Cross Road.'
Dr Timothy Leary, 1968

'It's becoming very clear that Charlie Manson is just a harmless freak, whose friends happened to indulge in fantasies about killing Sharon Tate.'
IT

Here Ends ELF

HI MOON

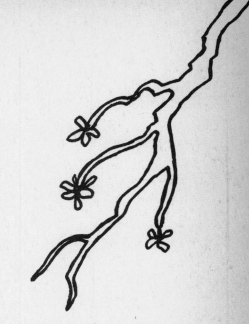

i don't know
if you've ever
looked at the moon
and thought
HI MOON
because it is quite high
at least
i was
when
i thought
of
this
?

ZEN WASHING UP

Hello plates!
You've had a busy day.
You're my mates!
There's nothing more to say.

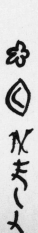

Some Bum Riffs of Life

ALLERGIES my favourite subject

Do you realize they had to kill a forest to make this book? And while you were reading that sentence, over four thousand people caught measles? And in the time it takes to say 'measles' five hundred acres of human skin have been infected by some kind of unpleasant rash? And that every year it gets more and more difficult to get any kind of reception on my telly?

Since the beginning of creation, everything in the world has been decaying and rotting, faster and faster. Animals are dying out. People are getting a lower and lower resistance to disease. Buildings are crumbling. Dustbins are all covered in slime and dust and germs. Yuck!

But that's not all. As people become more disease-ridden, they also become more paranoid and totally selfish. They get bigger and bigger life insurance policies – there are more life insurance policies now than at any other time in the history of Planet Earth. And more policemen. And more soldiers. And more pollution. And probably more spiders for all I know.

And as disease and insurance forms and policemen take over, it gets harder and harder for people to adapt to the shit, whether they're freaks, breadheads, straights or just complete bastards. In fact, some say that it's because the world is in such a state that everyone is turning into complete bastards, because, *everyone is developing allergies*.

Think of the dinosaurs, right? Look what happened to them. They got so big and cocky that they couldn't adapt to the shit any more and they started to develop all these allergies. So maybe you'd get a dinosaur sneezing every time it ran around a field or getting really nasty diarrhoea from eating a sandwich with white bread. And eventually they became allergic to each other and even to themselves. So they all died out because they couldn't adapt to the shit.

So the message for modern man is clear.

Adapt to the shit.

And don't think allergies are just eczema and wheezing in summer. I had a friend who couldn't adapt to the shit and he went around with the word, 'HATE' on his face with the skull and crossbones. Everybody thought it was a tattoo but it wasn't – it was an allergy coming through. And it can affect your behaviour too. My friend would suddenly turn to me and say, 'Fuck fuck fuck fuck off, Neil. I hate you, I gob on you, fuck you!' Luckily I realized this was just another allergy at work and so I didn't get upset, I just told him to avoid meat, vegetables and all liquids with a taste.

Of course, the media have just sussed that 'punk' was an allergy but that just shows how behind the media always are, right? *Of course,* punk's an allergy – because *everything is now allergic to everything*.

For instance, a lot of people who go into the rock business (or the music bizz, as some people call it) develop an allergy called 'legal hassles'. All bands eventually develop legal hassles but these days, they seem to be getting them more and more rapidly, like after their first single. Kajagoogoo had hardly appeared on *Top of the Pops* before they found they couldn't adapt to the shit and legal hassles got them.

The reason I know so much about the legal hassles allergy, is because I got into a heavy legal hassle once over a band I started up called Hawkwind. Everything was going fine until this guy came along telling us we had to get into contracts and vinyl and a world tour. I could see that I was going to get a really bad case of legal hassles. So it ended up with me having to sack the band right? Of course you'd never hear the *real* story in today's allergy-riddled music press.

People can develop allergies to anything in the world. You can be allergic to exams, to the television, to politics or even just to someone's aura. I know a few people who have become allergic to mine.

The first telltale sign that you've got an allergy is usually a little rash somewhere on your body. If you can spot this warning and identify it early on you may be able to avoid the bigger symptoms that come later on. *These diagrams may help you.*

1. Pimply and scaly
Allergic to: white sugar, sex, public transport, lentils (yes, this is actually possible!) and astrology.

2. Pale and spongy
Allergic to: air, relationships, human contact, any noise whatsoever, and solids.

3. Hot and sticky
Allergic to: *Wham*, legal hassles, curries, saturday night fever, warm climates, and central heating.

4. Swollen and Puffy
Allergic to: boring rice pudding, boring party political broadcasts, *One Man and his Dog*, masturbation, boring vibrations and the voidness of nothingness.

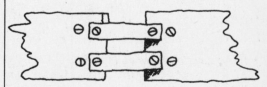

5. Rusty and Sore joints
Allergic to: Everything on Planet Earth. If you have this allergy, you are almost certainly an alien or a robot. The bad news is that, since you are basically inorganic and mechanical, you are going to find it hard to adapt to anything. So who knows what freaky symptoms you may develop now that we are in the age of Aquarius?

MY BROTHER GEOFF wears flared trousers and a gold medallion on his hairy chest. He always wears his shirt collar outside his jacket. He drives around in sports cars. Last year he went surfing in Australia when he was in South East Asia on a business trip.

MY BROTHER GEOFF is married and has two mortgages. One of them is three and the other is one and a half. But that doesn't stop him going out with 'the birds'. He drinks lots of alcohol and collects guns and knives.

MY BROTHER GEOFF is always trying to give me advice and telling me what music I should listen to. Once he hit me on the head and I've still got a slight scar. He thinks I should get a hairdryer so I could shape my hair like he does.

MY BROTHER GEOFF once built a nuclear reactor in our front room and polluted my whole family with fallout dust which my mum swept up and put in a jar on the mantlepiece. My dad thought it was really funny.

MY BROTHER GEOFF starts right-wing military coups in Central America for the CIA and invented a new kind of chemical warfare which he tried out on me and all my friends once when we were sitting around peacefully eating toasted marshmallows.

MY BROTHER GEOFF thinks I don't know that he started a holocaust which wiped out most of western civilisation and then floated up and destroyed the ozone layer so there was no organic life left at all on Planet Earth within twenty-five years.

MY BROTHER GEOFF will get very heavy and aggressive if there isn't at least one mention of him in my *Book of the Dead*.

Bla bla bla Brother Geoff.

AN AMAZINGLY BORING COINCIDENCE

Every guitar tells a tale. And mine goes on and on for ages and won't stop so I have to leave it outside in the hall if I want to get some sleep. You just have to look at all the stickers on a guitar or on a guitar case to know what sort of a tale it will probably tell.

In 1977 I lent my guitar to a guy called Dave the Hat. We called him that because he looked like a hat. I think that was why anyway.

Well Dave was just about to set off on some travels. He was going to hitch round Europe a bit and possibly if the bread lasted out he was going to go round the world as well. Like to places like Thailand to get put in prison for manufacturing bamboo bongs, or shoot down to Morocco on the Catch 22 dope bus then catch the Midnight Express ferry to South America to spend ten years on a herpes colony in Paraguay and then after training as a Buddhist monk end up felling trees in Canada because he knew some people in Ontario or Vancouver or somewhere.

Anyhow, none of this was to be . . . .

I told Dave that he couldn't travel anywhere if he didn't have a trusty box (i.e. guitar) with him, and he agreed with me and was about to cancel the whole trip. In the end I had to agree to lend him mine, but I've already told you that. It was stupid of me to lend it to him I suppose because I didn't have one then and I couldn't travel anywhere at all.

Well Dave got as far as a camp site somewhere between Paris and Calais when a *strange* and *amazing* thing happened . . . He lost my guitar.

I know because he sent me a weird postcard which said; 'I've lost your guitar already Neil. Still it means one less thing to carry. Dave.'

And that was the first in a whole chain of really weird things that happened. Soon after the weird postcard the second *strange* and *amazing* thing happened. We never heard from Dave again!

Fate was really spinning its pullover of confusion in our direction.

The next incredible spoke in this off-beat trail of subtle connections that seem so obvious and trivial years later but which at the time seem like a total blast of ignorance glue to the brain was that my guitar arrived back through the post covered in travel stickers! It had been to Australia, New Zealand, New Guinea, Newfoundland, New

York, Africa, Sri Lanka, Sweden and Spain, and was really conceited and full of itself if a bit undernourished. But no sign of Dave.

Maybe Dave hadn't made it to travel around the world, but my guitar certainly had. Maybe the truth is that my guitar *lost Dave* that time near Calais and decided to go off on the journey by itself.

Anyway by now there were loads of theories going round about what had happened to Dave. Some people said he was still in Calais, some thought he must have died. I mean his bread would never have lasted out that long.

So here is the final cog in this most *extraordinary* jigsaw. About this time there was a guy going around called Dave the Laugh, he was a different Dave from Dave the Hat, they called him Dave the Laugh so you wouldn't get them mixed up; and Dave the Laugh really liked making stupid bets with people all the time. Like how many buttons they had on their clothes and exactly when their guitar strings would break, and whether people would notice if you put your shoelace in their dinner and they ate it up. Stupid things like that.

Well, there were so many theories going round about what had happened to Dave the Hat, whether he was still alive or not, that Dave the Laugh decided to open a book on it. It was sort of like a book of the dead. And that's the *amazingly boring* coincidence. This is a Book of the Dead too, right?

And like I've told you all about Dave the Laugh's Book of the Dead in this Book of the Dead.

Weird!

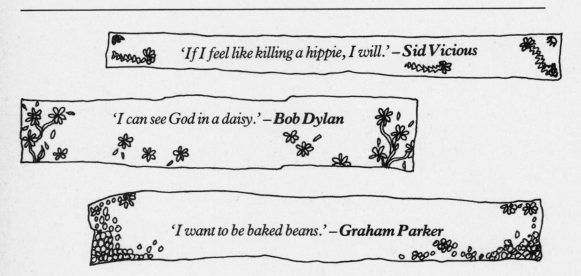

'If I feel like killing a hippie, I will.' – **Sid Vicious**

'I can see God in a daisy.' – **Bob Dylan**

'I want to be baked beans.' – **Graham Parker**

SURVIVAL IN .... STRAIGHT CITY AAAAAAAAARGH!!

OR how to stay completely beautiful when surrounded by a world of burnt out urban decay. Oh poor freaks of the world

There are so many methods of destruction, so many weapons.

How will you stay looking good with those terrible conglomerations of MAYA which have been put upon the earth to distract and dismay us?

How will the True Man, or his chick for that matter, survive and stay cool through these TORMENTS?

I'll try to tell you what I've learnt.....

Sometimes I wonder where Straight City came from. One day, there we were, the human race, beautiful, young, together – the next, the walls of Straight City were all around us.

And don't think it's easy to avoid it. You won't see signs around saying BEWARE STRAIGHT CITY AHEAD. The straights are too clever for that. No, you can be just wandering down the street, dreaming your dreams, humming your tunes, picking your nose – WHAM! – you're in Straight City.

But don't freak! Otherwise they'll suss you out and start behaving really hostilely. No, just go on down the street looking really normal – pick your nose, hum your tune but now you're not dreaming your dream. Every fibre of your body is on red alert. Sirens scream in your head. Men in orange overalls slide down poles. You move with the stealth of a leopard stalking through an alien, urban jungle. Your mind is racing.

You are ready for ANYTHING.

'Okay, Neil,' you say, 'that's fair enough as far as it goes. But what, in fact is wrong with Straight City?'

I'm very glad you asked me that because, if you hadn't, I wouldn't have been able to raise one of my giant pillows of wisdom:

ONCE
YOU
START
FEELING
AT HOME
IN
STRAIGHT
CITY
THEY
HAVE
GOT
YOU
YOU
ARE
NOW
A
STRAIGHT

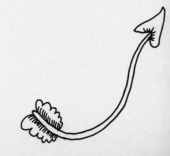

Yes, Straight City can get you whenever you are not on your guard – especially when you are entering places where straights are at their most dangerous.

At the disco

No normal people ever go to discos and even a few minutes of Shalamar, mirrors and horrible cocktails are about the heaviest trip that Straight City can lay on you. So here is my advice about discos:

Do not go to discos.

But let's assume you've been really stupid. Perhaps somebody double-dared you that you couldn't go to a disco, or you're writing a novel about a beautiful person caught up in a disco nightmare, or maybe you were just tricked into it.

You will not be welcomed at the door. They will not say, 'Hey, hello, nice to see you, man, come on in and groove with some really nice people.'

More likely, they'll just look at you as if you don't exist and say, 'All right, give us your hand.' And they don't want to do the special handshake! They'll just stamp your hand as if it was a pension book.

When you're in the disco, you'll find that nobody keeps still. They're all like cruising about, snapping their fingers and looking at themselves in the funny coloured mirrors they have there.

Do not do the same! It's incredibly dangerous – keeping time with a disco beat is how straights recharge their straight batteries. Disco is a straight energy source – even something like the Incredible String Band 12″ Disco Compilation.

So just sit down and blank out. If someone with a doormat on his chest and a lot of jewellery comes up behind you and says, 'What you drinking, babe,' don't panic. Just say, 'Excuse me, I don't believe in sexual stereotyping and anyway I'm not a chick, man. I'm a hippy.'

And don't smile. By now, he'll be feeling insecure about his masculinity and smiling at him could cause a very heavy scene.

If you're lucky, the place will start to clear as you mope about complaining that there's not any elderberry wine and asking the DJ if he's got any Third Ear Band albums. On the other hand, somebody might suddenly shout, 'Hey, everybody, get on down!'

When this happens, I like to play safe and hide under the table for the rest of the night, although quite a lot of the straights, as soon as someone says, 'Get down!', immediately get up.

Typical.

At the supermarket

A supermarket is one of the heaviest places you could imagine, which is why straights like hanging around there so much. If you've never been to one, really get your psychic strength together before you go.

The first thing you notice is the phosphorescent lighting that hurts your eyes. Then you hear someone playing Frank Ifield's greatest hits on the Hammond organ and it's coming at you from all sides. There are lots of television cameras everywhere and, now and then, there's a screen showing a big shop with some people in it. Oh no, something really horrible has come into shot. It's looking into the camera with wide, spaced-out eyes. You can see every hair up its horrible, gaping nostrils. It looks almost like – hey, it *is* me. Thank goodness for that.

You walk down a long corridor of stacked tins and dried cat food and special offer underarm deodorant and all you want is a toilet roll. You ask someone standing by a mountain of baked bean tins if they could tell you where the toilet rolls are but your voice sounds louder than it does normally. They stare at you as if you've just flashed in a church and the other shoppers whisper and point.

It's so long before you've found the toilet roll section that the man on the Hammond organ is halfway through a medley of David Essex hits by now.

In desperation, you look around for a packet that contains less than ten multicoloured, perfumed rolls in it. Finally you grab a family size one and make for the way out, where trained zombies stare into space and press tills, like in that film *I Was a Tesco Zombie.*

And you go to the till where there's no queue and the zombie says, 'One item only', and you say, 'Pardon?' and she looks at you really nastily and starts counting your toilet rolls at the top of her voice.

And everyone's looking at you now as if you were going to go away and smoke them. Or as if straights don't have bums at all.

On no – perhaps they don't.

At the hamburger joint

Okay, so you know it's bad for your karma but you've just got to have a hamburger. It's just one of those times when you need to taste blood and feel flesh tearing in your teeth. This means you will have to visit one of Straight City's holiest shrines, the hamburger joint.

To make you feel really hungry and glad you're alive, the straights have gone for a heavy marketing concept that will freak you out if you're not ready for it. They call the hamburger joint *Holocausts* and put sepia-tinted pictures of the bomb around the wall and there's milkshake called an ICBM, and Cruiseburgers served with hot napalm sauce.

Don't cry. Stay cool. If you're feeling really strong, try to get out a joke about nuclear fission chips. Then just order your meal – perhaps a Twenty Megadeath Cruiseburger, if you're really hungry – and get out of it as quickly and quietly as you can.

It's going to be some time before you'll want to go back there.

Crossing the road

You've been waiting at this zebra crossing for like half an hour, waiting for a vibe to get you across the road.

Straight City is all around you. A man asks you for the time. A dog looks at you really negatively. Some fascist six-year-olds laugh at your hair.

And you still haven't crossed the road. Now and then cars stop to let you cross and the drivers wave at you like they're having some kind of fit, which just freaks you out even more and you can't move.

What a terrible thing to happen. If you can't cross this road, it will be Straight City for sure. Your friends will say, 'Pity 'bout Neil. Straight City got him at a zebra crossing.'

So you just turn round, take off your shoes and walk backwards over the road like Paul McCartney on the front of *Abbey Road*.

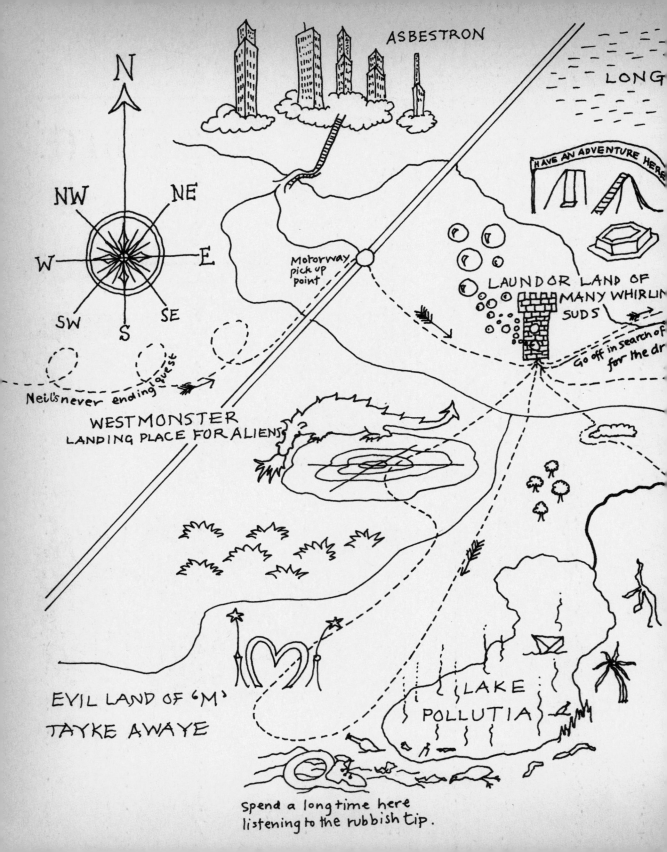

Things you can hear if you really listen.

Third Ear Reflections.

Press your ear to your pillow and you can hear a faraway rainstorm.

Put a piece of soap to your ear and you can hear whales crying.

Don't change your clothes for three weeks and you can hear mushrooms growing.

Think of a really difficult sum to do in your head and you can hear your braincells giving up and dying.

Put your ear to the ground in a park and you can hear worms singing as they work.

Put a glass to the wall, stick your ear against it, and you can hear the people upstairs fucking. Again!

What to do when you get sent a piece of dogshit in a jiffy bag.

Send off twenty three dog turds to twenty three friends of yours within twenty four hours of receiving the jiffy bag. Put your name at the bottom of a list of your friends and by the time your name is at the top of the list you should have had 40,926 dog turds posted to you!

And that's enough to grow food for three people for one and a half days except actually I think I may have got this wrong.

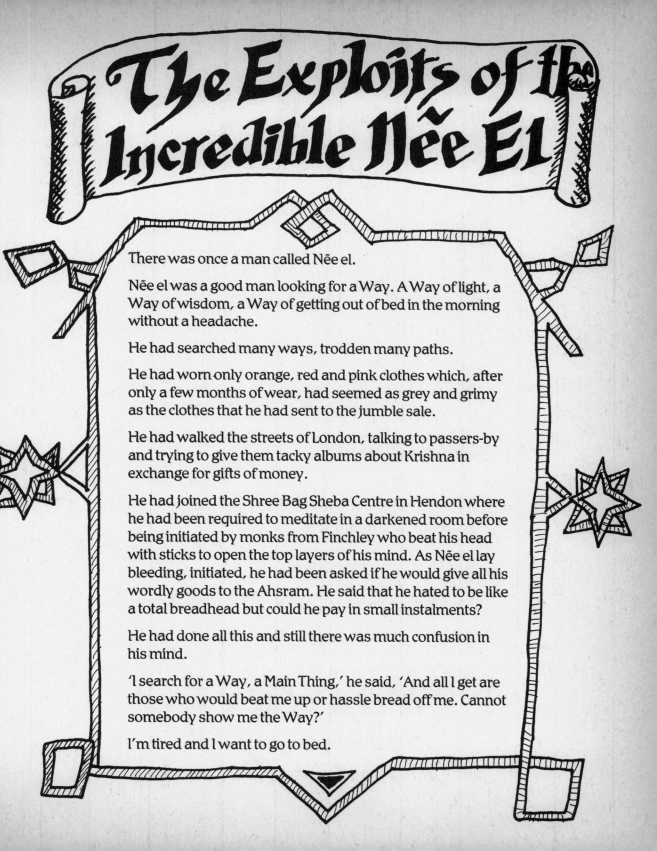

The Exploits of the Incredible Nẽe El

There was once a man called Nẽe el.

Nẽe el was a good man looking for a Way. A Way of light, a Way of wisdom, a Way of getting out of bed in the morning without a headache.

He had searched many ways, trodden many paths.

He had worn only orange, red and pink clothes which, after only a few months of wear, had seemed as grey and grimy as the clothes that he had sent to the jumble sale.

He had walked the streets of London, talking to passers-by and trying to give them tacky albums about Krishna in exchange for gifts of money.

He had joined the Shree Bag Sheba Centre in Hendon where he had been required to meditate in a darkened room before being initiated by monks from Finchley who beat his head with sticks to open the top layers of his mind. As Nẽe el lay bleeding, initiated, he had been asked if he would give all his wordly goods to the Ahsram. He said that he hated to be like a total breadhead but could he pay in small instalments?

He had done all this and still there was much confusion in his mind.

'I search for a Way, a Main Thing,' he said, 'And all I get are those who would beat me up or hassle bread off me. Cannot somebody show me the Way?'

I'm tired and I want to go to bed.

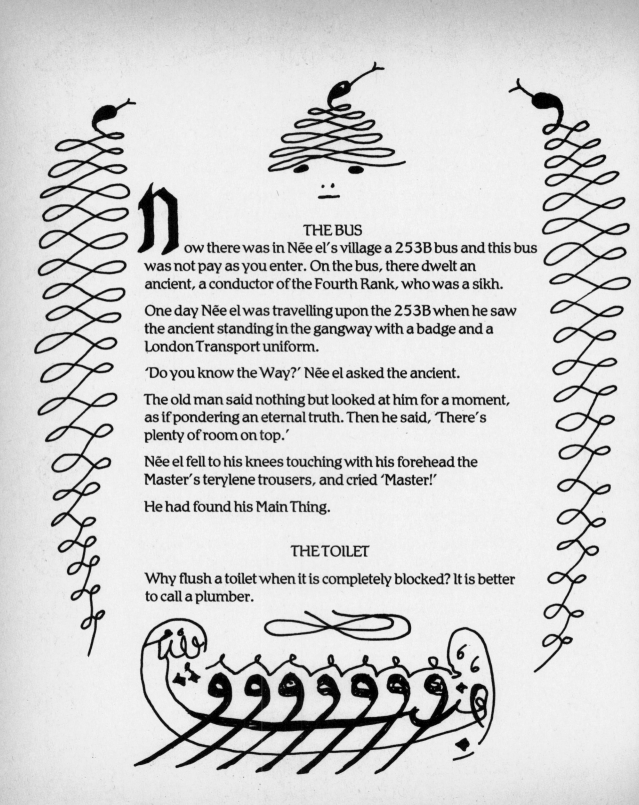

THE BUS

Now there was in Nēe el's village a 253B bus and this bus was not pay as you enter. On the bus, there dwelt an ancient, a conductor of the Fourth Rank, who was a sikh.

One day Nēe el was travelling upon the 253B when he saw the ancient standing in the gangway with a badge and a London Transport uniform.

'Do you know the Way?' Nēe el asked the ancient.

The old man said nothing but looked at him for a moment, as if pondering an eternal truth. Then he said, 'There's plenty of room on top.'

Nēe el fell to his knees touching with his forehead the Master's terylene trousers, and cried 'Master!'

He had found his Main Thing.

THE TOILET

Why flush a toilet when it is completely blocked? It is better to call a plumber.

STARS IN A FRYING-PAN

So great was Nêe el's desire to find his Main Thing that he stayed with the ancient for many months, and studied his ways. Where the sage went, there would also go Nêe el.

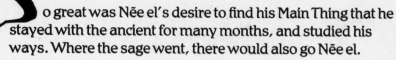

Their journey took them through several pubs, the launderette and always the old man would go quietly about his business, occasionally staring at Nêe el as if to say, 'Who the fuck *are* you?'

Often he would travel upon the 253B and speak to other novices of the order travelling upon the bus. He explained to them the Alphabetical Fares Grading System which none but he and the Ministry of Transport understood or cared about. He told them how, by staring at posters for Red Rover passes, they could make their minds go completely blank.

And when the ancient came to collect the fares, he would cry out in a loud voice, 'Behold the Master! Behold the Way!'

Although many novices travelled upon the 253B, none would stay for long and some left after only one fare stop.

But Nêe el would follow the Master wherever he went. He would sit in his garden, watching the ancient with his family, in front the television or cleaning his Fiesta.

Once, summoning his courage, Nêe el knocked on the door at the Master's house and asked him for a pearl of wisdom.

The Master said nothing but raised the frying-pan that he was carrying high in the air and brought it down upon Nêe el's head.

Nêe el experienced an astonishing blinding flash and saw stars in the firmament. When he awoke from his trance, it was night time.

'Thank you, Master' he said, but the Master had gone.

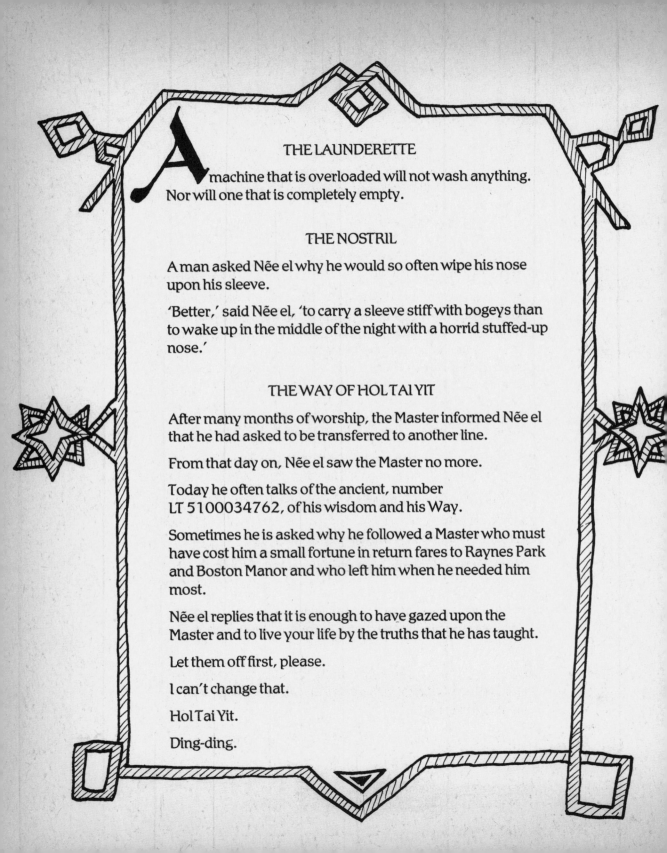

THE LAUNDERETTE

A machine that is overloaded will not wash anything. Nor will one that is completely empty.

THE NOSTRIL

A man asked Nēe el why he would so often wipe his nose upon his sleeve.

'Better,' said Nēe el, 'to carry a sleeve stiff with bogeys than to wake up in the middle of the night with a horrid stuffed-up nose.'

THE WAY OF HOL TAI YIT

After many months of worship, the Master informed Nēe el that he had asked to be transferred to another line.

From that day on, Nēe el saw the Master no more.

Today he often talks of the ancient, number LT 5100034762, of his wisdom and his Way.

Sometimes he is asked why he followed a Master who must have cost him a small fortune in return fares to Raynes Park and Boston Manor and who left him when he needed him most.

Nēe el replies that it is enough to have gazed upon the Master and to live your life by the truths that he has taught.

Let them off first, please.

I can't change that.

Hol Tai Yit.

Ding-ding.

A Message from Jefferson Starship

" 'STARSHIP STARSHIP STARSHIP
People (people!) Needed Now
EARTH GETTING TOO THICK
All positions open: captains, astral navigators, cooks, dancers,
energy centres. We need experts in explosives, wave
mechanics, laser technics, atomic and trionic physics, labrian
tantronics, telemetry etc. Telepaths, machinists, chemists,
woodworkers, physicians, craftsmen, poets, artists, recording
engineers, *moon pair*, and particularly people who don't have
any idea what they're all about.
If it seems your head is into this please write and talk about
something for a bit.
You will not be contacted for a bit.
Please just prepare your minds and your bodies. Experiment —
move your mind. Practise telepathy and kinesis — if you feel it.
JOIN US — A PLUNGE INTO REALITY.' "

Sixth Bobo

Leonardcohensushi

Leonard Cohen

The only writer who understands.

This is a bit of the book I would have liked to have written
myself but Leonard Cohen already did.

Shit.

Even the title speaks eternal truth.

Beautiful Losers

Take it away, Leonard.

Beautiful Losers

by Leonard Cohen

O God, Your Morning Is Perfect. People Are Alive In Your World. I Can Hear The Little Children In The Elevator. The Airplane Is Flying Through The Original Blue Air. Mouths Are Eating Breakfast. The Radio Is Filled With Electricity. The Trees Are Excellent. You Are Listening To The Voices Of The Faithless Who Tarry On The Bridge Of Spikes. I Have Let Your Spirit Into The Kitchen. The Westclock Is Also Your Idea. The Government Is Meek. The Dead Do Not Have To Wait. You Comprehend Why Someone Must Drink Blood. O God, This Is Your Morning. There Is Music Even From A Human Thigh-Bone Trumpet. The Ice-Box Will Be Forgiven. I Cannot Think Of Anything Which Is Not Yours. The Hospitals Have Drawers Of Cancer Which They Do Not Own. The Mesozoic Waters

Abounded With Marine Reptiles Which Seemed Eternal. You Know The
Details Of The Kangaroo. Place Ville Marie Grows And Falls Like A Flower
In Your Binoculars. There Are Old Eggs In The Gobi Desert. Nausea Is An
Earthquake In Your Eye. Even The World Has A Body. We Are Watched
Forever. In The Midst Of Molecular Violence The Yellow Table Clings To
Its Shape. I Am Surrounded By Members Of Your Court. I Am Frightened
That My Prayer Will Fall Into My Mind. Somewhere This Morning Agony
Is Explained. The Newspaper Says That A Human Embryo Was Found
Wrapped In A Newspaper And That A Doctor Is Suspected. I Am Trying To
Know You In The Kitchen Where I Sit. I Fear My Small Heart. I Cannot
Understand Why My Arm Is Not A Lilac Tree. I Am Frightened Because
Death Is Your Idea. Now I Do Not Think It Behoves Me To Describe Your
World. The Bathroom Door Is Opening By It Self And I Am Shivering With
So Much Fear. O God, I Believe Your Morning Is Perfect. Nothing Will
Happen Incompletely. O God, I Am Alone In The Desire Of My Education
But A Greater Desire Must Be Lodged With You. I Am A Creature In Your
Morning Writing A Lot Of Words Beginning With Capitals. Seven-Thirty In
The Ruin Of My Prayer. I Sit Still In Your Morning While Cars Drive Away.
O God, If There Are Fiery Journeys Be With Edith As She Climbs. Be With
F. If He Has Earned Himself Agony. Be With Catherine Who Is Dead Three
Hundred Years. Be With Us In Our Ignorance And Our Wretched
Doctrines. We Are All Of Us Tormented With Your Glory. You Have
Caused Us To Live On The Crust Of A Star. F. Suffered Horribly In His
Last Days. Catherine Was Mangled Every Hour In Mysterious Machinery.
Edith Cried In Pain. Be With Us This Morning Of Your Time. Be With Us
At Eight O'Clock Now. Be With Me As I Lose The Crumbs Of Grace. Be
With Me As The Kitchen Comes Back. Please Be With Me Especially While
I Poke Around The Radio For Religious Music. Be With Me In The Phases
Of My Work Because My Brain Feels Like It Has Been Whipped And I
Yearn To Make A Small Perfect Thing Which Will Live In Your Morning

Like Curious Static Through A President's Elegy Or A Nude Hunchback Acquiring A Tan On The Crowded Oily Beach. Is All The World A Prayer To Some Star? Are All The Years Of The World A Catalogue Of The Events Of Some Holiday? Do All Things Happen At Once? Is There A Needle In The Haystack? Do We Perform In The Twilight Before A Vast Theatre Of Empty Stone Benches? Do We Hold Hands With Our Grandfathers? Are They Warm And Royal, The Rags Of Death? Are All The People Living At This Very Second Fingerprinted? Is Beauty The Pulley? How Are The Dead Received In The Expanding Army? Is It True That There Are No Wallflowers At The Dance? May I Love The Forms Of Girls Instead Of Licking Labels? May I Die A Little At The Uncovering Of Unfamiliar Breasts? May I Raise A Path Of Goosepimples With My Tongue? May I Hug My Friend Instead Of Working? Are Sailors Naturally Religious? May I Squeeze A Golden-Haired Thigh Between My Legs And Feel Blood Flowing And Hear The Holy Tick Of The Fainting Clock? Could It Be Recorded In The Books Of Some Law That Shit Is Kosher? Is There A Difference In Dreaming Geometry And Bizarre Sex Positions? Is The Epileptic Always Graceful? Is There Such A Thing As Waste? Is It Wonderful To Think About An Eighteen-Year-Old Girl Wearing Tight Jelly Underwear? Does Love Visit Me When I Pump Myself? O God, There Is A Scream, All The Systems Are Screaming. I Am Locked In A Fur Store But I Believe You Want To Steal Me. Does Gabriel Trip A Burglar Alarm? Why Was I Sewn Into Bed With The Nymphomaniac? Am I Easy To Pluck As A Spear Of Grass? O God, I Love So Many Things It Will Need Years To Take Them Away One By One. I Adore Thy Details. Why Have You Let Me See The Bare Ankle Tonight In The Treehouse? Why Did You Vouchsafe Unto Me A Minute Flash Of Desire? May I Unfasten My Loneliness And Collide Once Again With A Beautiful Greedy Body? May I Fall Asleep After A Soft Happy Kiss? May I Have A Dog For A Pet? May I Teach Myself To Be Handsome? May I Pray At All?

Seventh Bobo

The Retinal Circus

Do not proceed past this bobo unless you don't mind going mad.

You've got to be really serious about reading this book if you're going to go any further, okay?

All right. Well, don't say I didn't warn you . . .

In this stage, you will find your whole life flashing before you under your eyelids or, if you're good at hallucinating or are really drunk, on the wall.

When I reached this stage and my life started flashing before me, it was really embarrassing. In fact, now you've reached this stage, you might see my life flashing around somewhere too so I might as well confess to you now some of the most embarrassing things that have ever happened to me.

True Confessions

The True Confessions of Neil in the Seventh Bobo

I once went to a party at my chick's friend's father's work in a suit.

I once wanked into my grandfather's Wellington boots and he never even noticed.

I passed O Level economics.

I used to pretend I was Meatloaf to try and get into parties.

I once got Steve Hillage's autograph and sold it.

I listen to 'Down Your Way' on Radio Four.

I once clubbed a spider to death with *The Autobiography of a Yogi*.

I once pretended to hallucinate after half a glass of advocaat.

My Whole Life Flashing Before You

My Whole Life Flashing Before You.

My dog I had as a kid. It was a Sagittarian and, like all Sagittarians, was continually questing and sniffing.

The place on the towpath where I lost my stash

John and Kim practising intuitive massage.

My college. At least, it's somewhere around here I think.

Living totally self-sufficiently on the Social Security in Wales.

The only time I was ever in the papers.

Someone's Aura

A magic white dog turd.

"Oh Ken,
I've known you since you were ten,
And you were a fucking bastard then,
Ken."

A friend of mine Ken who hates me.

Letters to my chick.

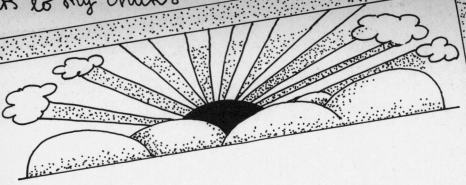

Sweet lady –
Hey d'you know it was only four solstices ago that we were together, as one in nature, grooving to the most far-out sunset you would ever believe? You remember, we just took off together and escaped from the concrete nightmare to somewhere magical, celtic and pagan? And when we caught *Fantasia* at the Pontypool Odeon, the straights threw us out 'cos we were freaking to its heavy images? And then it started to rain so we had to take the bus home because I was feeling a little chesty?

Hey, what a weekend that was! Beautiful times!

I'm in a great squat down here but we're having a lot of bread hassles. D'you remember the day before you left, I did the shopping? Well, I don't think you ever paid me for your share of the Rice Crispies. I don't want to be a total breadhead or anything but please remember our agreement. 'Nuff said!

Hey, I miss you my little lady. Your face, your tambourine, your cooking . . .

It's never too late to have a happy childhood.

Your lief-mate

PS It was a large family-sized pack.

sunrise notepaper. © n

Hey sweet chick –

Okay, so you sold out – did the whole breadhead trip. You call it account manager at an advertising agency? I call it arch-conspirator in the military-industrial complex, okay?

And why the heavy humour trip about my erection problem (which you promised never to mention)?

You know what I think? I think *you're* the one with the problem. Performance isn't everything you know! You can't collect orgasms like stamps at the supermarket. Maybe your crowd goes in for acquiring the latest hatch-back, wall-to-wall, fitted stereo orgasms but that just shows how straight you are!

Because where I'm coming from, there's a whole new way of sex. We make love with the whole body – we're against any kind of genital sex, which is total sexual fascism, the tyranny of private parts. That's what makes someone like me the perfect new lover – tender, warm and totally uninterested in anything except watercolours and astrology.

Anyway, thanks for sending me the box of your precious new 'product' Blubber Crunch to make up for the Rice Crispies. I think I'm developing a habit and the guys from the local branch of the Stop Making Sweets Out Of Endangered Species League cleaned me out last night. Could you send me a few more packets?

It's never too late to have a happy childhood.

Your lief-mate

ne il

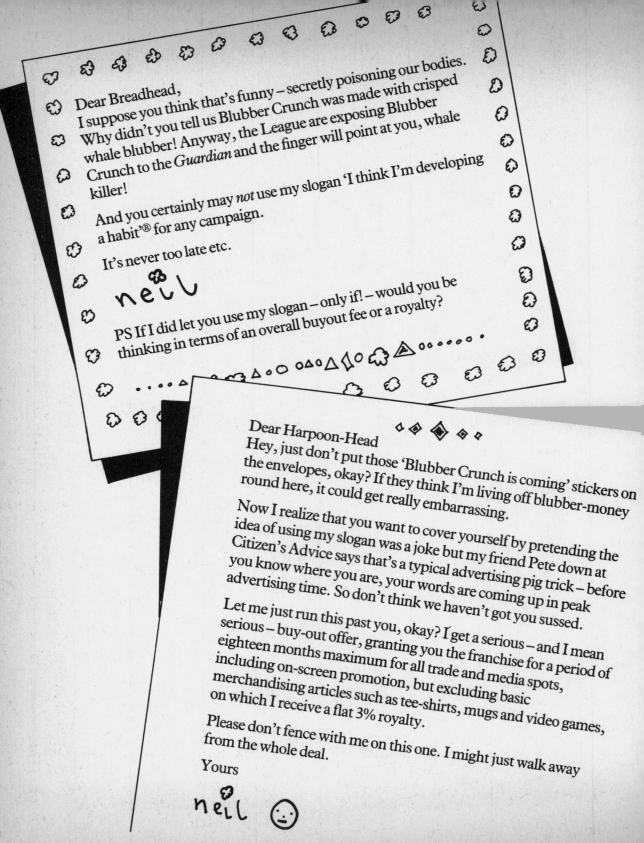

Dear Breadhead,

I suppose you think that's funny – secretly poisoning our bodies. Why didn't you tell us Blubber Crunch was made with crisped whale blubber! Anyway, the League are exposing Blubber Crunch to the *Guardian* and the finger will point at you, whale killer!

And you certainly may *not* use my slogan 'I think I'm developing a habit'® for any campaign.

It's never too late etc.

neil

PS If I did let you use my slogan – only if! – would you be thinking in terms of an overall buyout fee or a royalty?

Dear Harpoon-Head

Hey, just don't put those 'Blubber Crunch is coming' stickers on the envelopes, okay? If they think I'm living off blubber-money round here, it could get really embarrassing.

Now I realize that you want to cover yourself by pretending the idea of using my slogan was a joke but my friend Pete down at Citizen's Advice says that's a typical advertising pig trick – before you know where you are, your words are coming up in peak advertising time. So don't think we haven't got you sussed.

Let me just run this past you, okay? I get a serious – and I mean serious – buy-out offer, granting you the franchise for a period of eighteen months maximum for all trade and media spots, including on-screen promotion, but excluding basic merchandising articles such as tee-shirts, mugs and video games, on which I receive a flat 3% royalty.

Please don't fence with me on this one. I might just walk away from the whole deal.

Yours

neil ☺

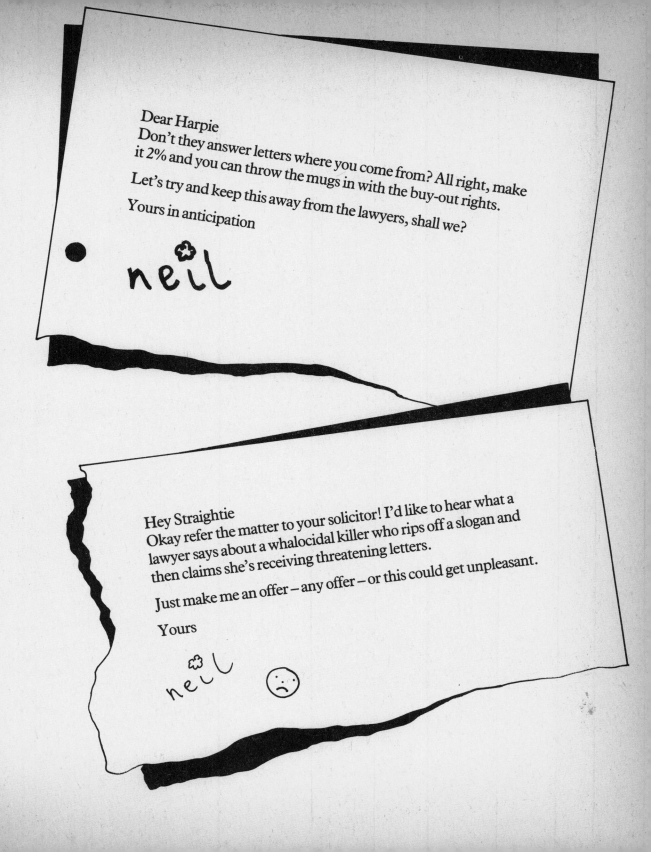

Dear Harpie
Don't they answer letters where you come from? All right, make it 2% and you can throw the mugs in with the buy-out rights.

Let's try and keep this away from the lawyers, shall we?

Yours in anticipation

neil

Hey Straightie
Okay refer the matter to your solicitor! I'd like to hear what a lawyer says about a whalocidal killer who rips off a slogan and then claims she's receiving threatening letters.

Just make me an offer – any offer – or this could get unpleasant.

Yours

neil

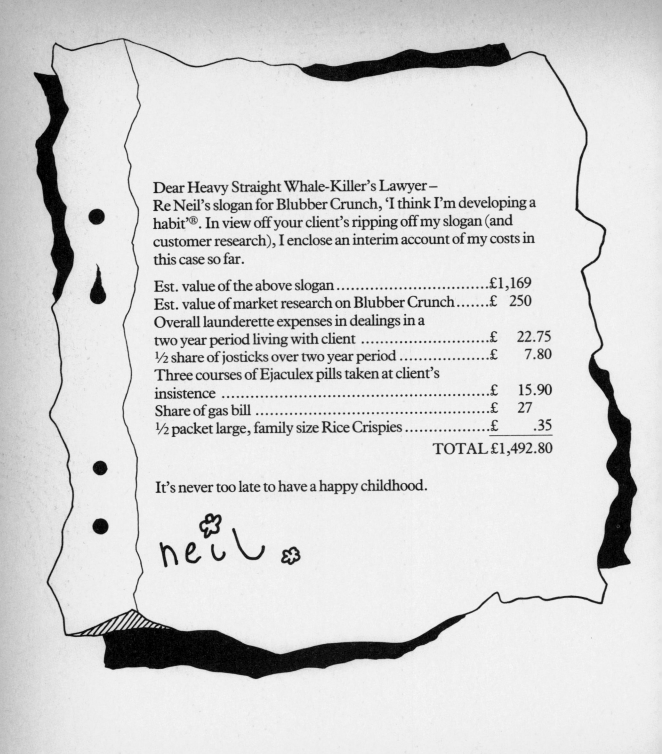

Dear Heavy Straight Whale-Killer's Lawyer –
Re Neil's slogan for Blubber Crunch, 'I think I'm developing a habit'®. In view off your client's ripping off my slogan (and customer research), I enclose an interim account of my costs in this case so far.

Est. value of the above slogan £1,169
Est. value of market research on Blubber Crunch.......£ 250
Overall launderette expenses in dealings in a
two year period living with client ....£ 22.75
½ share of josticks over two year period ....£ 7.80
Three courses of Ejaculex pills taken at client's
insistence ....£ 15.90
Share of gas bill ....£ 27
½ packet large, family size Rice Crispies ....£ .35
                                                        TOTAL £1,492.80

It's never too late to have a happy childhood.

neil

TUNNEL VISION

hurdy gurdy mushroom man
has locked me in a frying pan
and everybody laughs at me
the frozen scarecrow in the sea
a gypsy girl with golden hair
that shouts at me when I'm not there
and then I look and see I'm not
it makes me wonder quite a lot
and all the fishes swim away
and say don't hassle us today
and suddenly a voice appears
and wipes away the sheepdog fears
of all the people here with me
and will my auntie come for tea
I promise you that I'm not stoned
and will you leave my space alone
and what is going on round here
when words like these are what you hear
and no one takes it seriously
and people come and hassle me
and try to stop me writing it
as if I didn't know it's shit.

THE PRACTICAL PAGAN

The Breadhead Conspiracy has put it about that New-Age Paganists spend solstice after solstice worshipping trees and trying to get in touch with the spirit of Aleister Crowley and Jim Morrison. In other words, that we're out of touch with so-called reality.

But pagans aren't stupid, you know. We realise that everyday straight life has to continue in the normal way – at least until the time of Ragnavok when Baldur of Asgard will materialise and the Egnoks will come down to Obrogan. In fact, in many ways, the New-Age Pagans are very advanced when it comes to survival in the heavy, modern world.

Here are some practical hints:

Channel selection by dowsing

Okay, so the *Old Grey Whistle Test's* are on one side and *Bastard Squad's* on the other. How to make the cosmic choice? Allow your dowsing stick to hang over the television set. A twitch to the left means you should turn to BBC, to the right ITV. If it swings wildly to the left and then rapidly back to the status quo, check out what's on Channel 4.

Weather forecast by natural phenomena

Follow the age-old Pagan's country code. For example:
If dustbin men are rather surly, it's been pissing down since very early.
If all seems white when you're a-rising, a snowfall would not be surprising.
If the sky is green with stripes of red, you must be stoned out of your head.
If nuclear bombs should come at all, a hard rain's a-gonna fall.

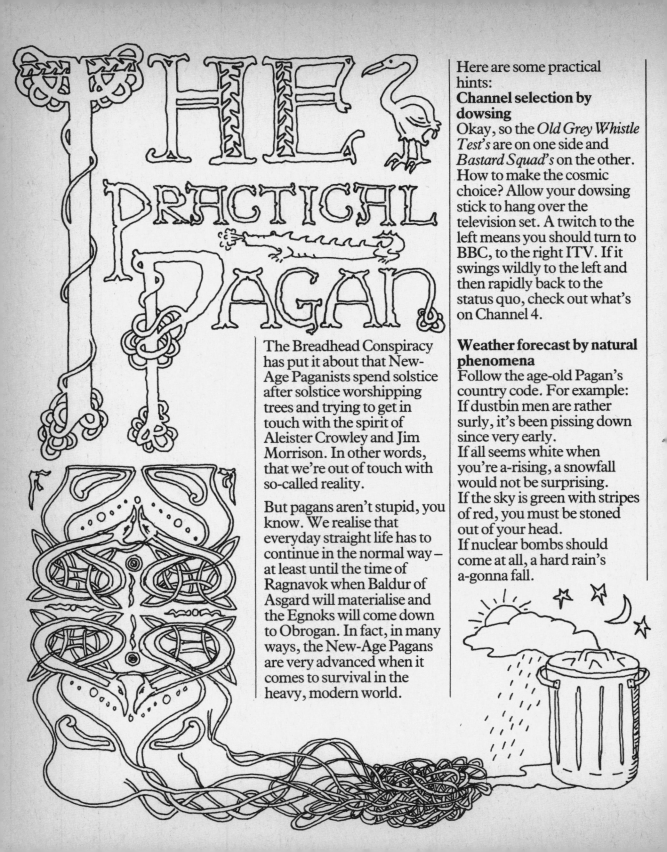

Telling the time by Tarot

For example. 'What's the time, Neil?'

I ask the questioner to shuffle the pack thoroughly. I then cut the pack and ask the questioner to take the top card and place it at the bottom of the pack. When the questioner has done this, I ask him or her to take the third card from the top and lay it on the table. This is the Time Card.

Now, I see that one of the Major Arcana cards has been selected so straight away I know that we are into the Winter Solstice. I cut now to the Second Time Card which tells me that someone very close to the questioner will die very shortly. However, since this was not what the questioner asked me about it, I reveal only that, since the card is the Hanged Man, it is now almost certainly early in *Samhain*.

Finally I turn the Third Time Card to reveal an ace in the Suit of Wand which tells the full answer to me.

'It is some time in the evening, quite early in December.'
'Thank you very much, Neil.'

Answerphone by Celtick Talking Sticks

Magick Celtick sticks, which can be purchased at any well-stocked pagan store, will tell a tale of mythic celtic lore if thrown so that they land in one of the mystick patterns. Before you go out, throw the sticks into a mystick pattern near the phone. If the phone rings, vibrations will reach it and, if your caller is another pagan or Celt, he or she will know you are out on a hunting and gathering mission.

Gas meter feeding by Runic lore

Gather the Runic pieces around you on the floor and place in the centre of them one 50p piece. Find the runic pieces that most closely resemble the coin and, one by one, place them underneath it. Then take a sharp knife and craft the rune into the shape of a coin. Finally, insert the carved runic piece into the gas meter.

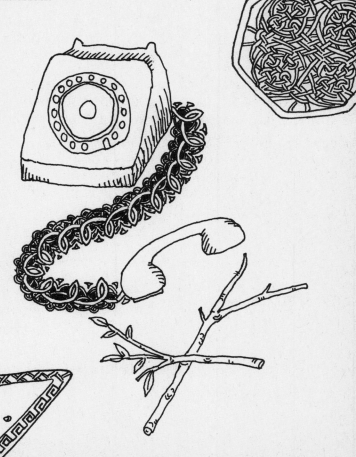

Dear Channel Four,

Here is a script that I wrote for you last night. It's called *Ooh my Back!* I think it would make a really good sitcom on TV.

PS This is the only copy, right, so...I want it back okay? And you better not rip off any of the ideas and characters in it either.

Dear Mr Neil,

Please find enclosed your script of *Ooh my Back* which we have read. Due to lack of funds and airtime we are unable to place it at present. Thank you for your interest.

Hey come on!
I thought Channel Four was meant to be like the People's Channel? Maybe the breadheads got there first again! Look, since I sent you that script a lot of stuff in it has started to come up on TV right? And just because you sent the script back to me doesn't mean you couldn't have had it photocopied first right? I'm not that stupid. And I don't want to be like a breadhead but I should be getting royalties for all that.
PS Can you reply a bit quicker this time because I might not be at this address much longer.

OOH MY BACK

by Neil Weedon Watkins-Pie

Dave   Hello darling I'm home. I had a really freaky day at the office.

Rose   Hello darling can I fix you a joint?

Dave   No it's all right I'll do it. Oh Wow! Who's been at my stash?

Rose   Oh darling, I forgot to tell you, I told the kids they could have the seeds to play with in the garden, and well...that's what your stash was...mostly seeds.

Dave   Oh fuck darling, that's bullshit, there were at least two flowers left and where's my bit of black that was in there as well? Oh no, I forgot to tell you, my boss is coming round to dinner tonight, what are we going to do? We won't be able to turn him on now.

Rose   Huh! Men! You expect me to be able to conjure up a freakout high from nowhere at a moment's notice.

Dave   Yes, I know, I'm sorry darling. It is a bit unfair of me. I have been a bit rough on you lately.

(THEY SNOG)
DING DONG

Dave   Oh no, that can't be him already!

Rose   No, look it's Jack the next door neighbour.

Jack   Hello Dave, hello Rose.

Dave and
Rose   Hello Jack.

Jack   Look Dave, Rose, I'm sorry to trouble you but I just popped round to see if you could help me out, you see I'm in a bit of a spot.

Dave   Yes?

Jack   I've got my boss coming over to dinner tonight and I've completely run out of drugs. Do you think I could just borrow a couple of joints worth, I'll pay you back, honest.

Dave and
Rose   Oh no! That's torn it! Looks like we're in for a pretty heavy evening. HWA HWA HWAAAAAAAA.

Scene 2
LATER ON THAT EVENING
DAVE'S BOSS IS SITTING AT THE DINING ROOM TABLE. THEY'VE JUST FINISHED EATING.

Boss   Well that was a lovely alfalfa casserole Rose.

Rose   Oh no, it was terrible really because I made it. I'll just clear it all up and mope around a bit.

Dave   That's right. Er, would you like a joint…Sir?

Boss   Oh yes, Dave, what a far out idea.

Dave   Here it is. (HE LIGHTS IT).

Boss   (TAKING A PUFF) Oh yes, very nice.

Dave   That's enough (DAVE SNATCHES THE JOINT OUT OF HIS BOSS'S

HAND AND RUSHES TO THE FRONT DOOR). I've just got to nip next door, I'll be back in a minute.

IN THE NEIGHBOUR'S HOUSE, JACK'S BOSS IS JUST FINISHING HIS DINNER, TOO.

Boss 2   Well, thank you, Mrs Jack that really was a lovely meat stew.

Jill   Oh no, it was nothing, you sexy thing you.

Jack   Er, would you like a smoke Sir?

Boss 2   I don't mind if I do.

(THERE IS AN EMBARRASSING PAUSE, THEN A KNOCK AT THE DOOR).

Jack   (RUNS TO ANSWER IT, IT IS DAVE). You took your time, didn't you?

Dave   I'm sorry Jack.

Jack   Did you bring the stuff?

Dave   I've got this (SHOWS JACK THE ALREADY LIT JOINT).

Jack   Is that all?

Dave   I'm sorry Jack, the kids have nicked the rest.

Jack   Well, give it here. (JACK GOES BACK TO THE TABLE). Would you like that smoke now Sir?

Boss 2   Oh rather.

Jack   (GIVES HIM THE JOINT). Here you are.

Boss 2   Oh wow, about time too. Thank you. (BOSS 2 TAKES AN ENORMOUS DRAG).

Dave   Oh no, Jack! Jack, come over here.

Jack   Take as much as you want Sir (ASIDE) Not now Dave!

Dave   Can I speak to you a moment Jack?

Jack   Oh alright. (TO BOSS) Excuse me Sir.

Dave   Listen, I don't know how to say this but can you hustle that joint back off him because I'm also having my boss round to dinner and he wants to get smashed as well!

Jack   Oh no! Heavy! I can't just hustle the joint off him. He'll never give me any promotion, you'll just have to wait.

Dave   But...Oh no...

Boss 2   Jack my boy this really is a mighty fine joint you know. (HE TAKES ANOTHER REALLY LONG DRAG). (MEANWHILE BACK AT DAVE'S HOUSE).

Boss 1   Where has Dave gone with that joint?

Rose   Oh well, I think he just popped next door to er...to look after his pussy...

Boss 1   His pussy? I didn't know he was like that.

Rose   Oh yes.

Boss 1   Why don't you give me a blow job now instead?

Rose   Oh...alright.

(DAVE COMES BACK JUST IN TIME.)

Dave   Oh hello Sir.

Boss 1   Where's that joint Dave?

Dave   Well, Sir, I, the thing is, Jack said, Oh never mind, I'll just go back and get it.

(BACK AT JACK'S HOUSE)

Boss 2   Boy, oh boy, I really am stoned.
(DAVE RUNS IN AND SNATCHES THE JOINT OUT OF HIS HAND AND DASHES STRAIGHT OUT AGAIN).

Dave   Sorry Jack...

Jack   Well of all the...

Boss 2   Well I...well you won't be getting any promotion now Jack I can tell you.

(BACK AT DAVE'S).

Boss 1   Where were we?

(IN RUNS DAVE).

Dave   Here's the joint Sir.

Boss 1   Thanks Dave (HE PUFFS). What? This is just roach now, what's going on?

Dave   Oh no!

Boss 1   Well you won't be getting any promotion now either, I can tell you.

HWA HWA HWAAAAAAAA.

Eighth Bobo

External Game Reality

At this stage, you, the voyager in search of Truth, may have become aware that, although we are minute specks of dust in the stratosphere of the cosmos, humdrum everyday things like the bathtub ring or a broken zip or Frank Bough still hang around, annoying you and trying to kid you that they actually exist! Huh!

These are just EXTERNAL GAME REALITIES, or the games of life. The best way of dealing with them is not to get freaked by them – just *play* them.

HORIZONTAL T'AI CHI

The art of getting your body together without getting out of bed

T'ai Chi is an ancient martial art which ancient warriors used to kill each other with, while at the same time reaching a higher spiritual plane. These days the killing part is like optional but a lot of people have discovered that it's a great way of keeping in trim without getting out of bed. And it's something we can all do in the state where scientists say we spend over 90 per cent of our time – asleep.

Each of these Horizontal T'ai Chi positions tells you something about your character and state of mind so that, as you move around in your sleep, you're toning up your body and, if you can get someone to watch and take pictures, you can work out where your head is at too.

The First Stage

To practise Horizontal T'ai Chi, it is essential that you empty your thoughts and are in a state of complete relaxation and readiness. The best way to achieve this is to take a good handful of whatever downers you can hit your doctor for. Most doctors are pretty good about prescribing these sort of drugs to people so you shouldn't have too much difficulty. If you're unlucky, try another doctor or several other doctors and make up a really heavy cocktail.

The Second Stage

You should now be slipping into what we call 'The Twilight Zone'. If at this stage you feel like clutching the bed-post, do so if it helps. Do *not* resist as you slip into unconsciousness – the experts say you should adopt about thirty T'ai Chi positions every night and, if for any reason you miss some of the early positions, your partner should wake you and make you start again.

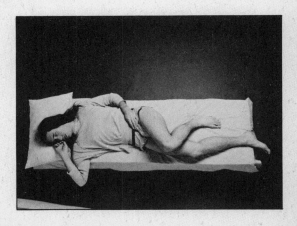

HORIZONTAL T'AI CHI

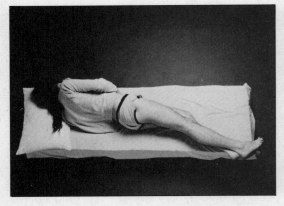

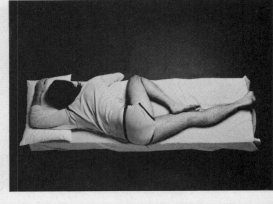

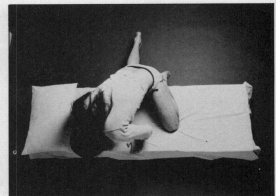

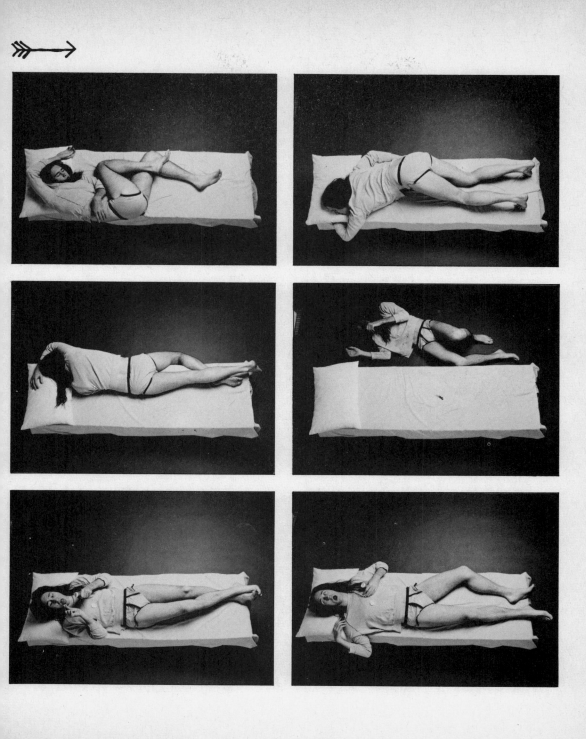

Neil's non-pop up page.

Mandala of my mind

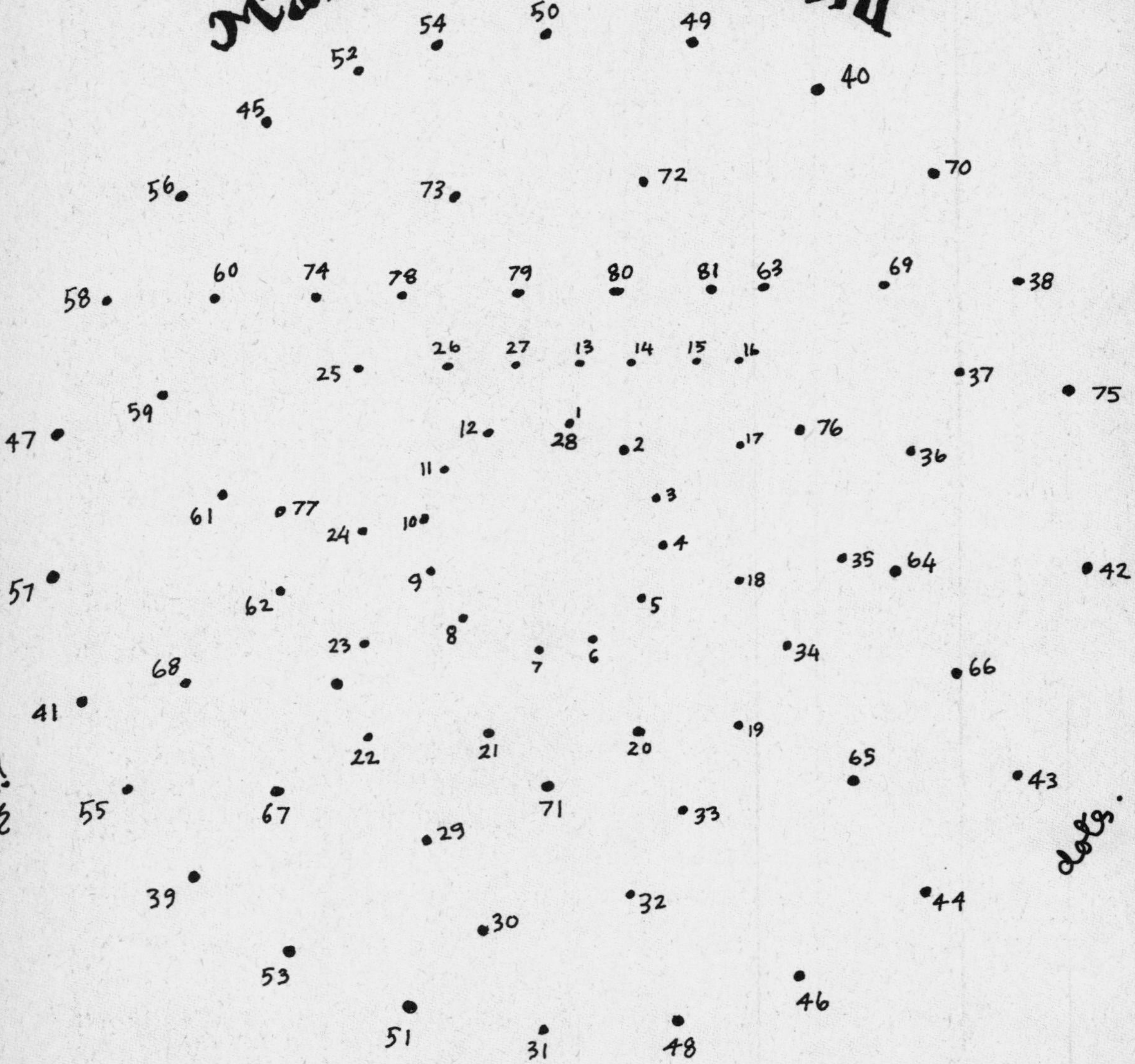

52 54 50 49

45 40

56 73 72 70

58 60 74 78 79 80 81 63 69 38

25 26 27 13 14 15 16 37 75

59 12 1 2 17 76 36

47 11 28

61 77 10 3

24 9 4 35 64 42

57 62 18 5

23 8 34

68 7 6 66

41 19

22 21 20 65 43

55 67 71 33

39 29 44

53 30 32

46

51 31 48

join up the dots.

In this picture there are thirteen clues which, if you work them out correctly, will tell you the whereabouts of hidden treasure which I buried in a cake tin somewhere in the British Isles. In the cake tin are a hand knitted pixie cap, my stash, a roach end, my shades and I think I left a book of mine there too.

P.S. If you do find it, could you give me the shades and the book back because I can't remember where it is myself now and some of the thirteen hidden clues are really difficult....At least I think it was thirteen.

Ninth Bobo

The Blast of Swooning.

This is the Ninth Bobo and it's a pretty heavy and scary one. We don't want to spend too much time here, okay?

It's heavy because the number nine is like an upside down six and, if you had three copies of this *Book of the Dead* and put them together, upside down, open at this page that would make the number –

666

And that's the number of the DEVIL!
Never try dialling this number on your telephone or you might get an evil emergency ambulance coming round to collect your soul with its demon siren blaring, or you could get a satanic fire engine with a hose that spouts flames. Hang on a minute. . . . Oh no! HEAVEEEEEEE! We're running out of space now and I haven't done the last four Bobos and I'm going to have to leave this *Book of the Dead* on Bobo Nine! That's incredible bad luck. You'll never know how to complete the spiritual journey and you'll be stuck here in Limbo No 9 for ever and ever. Oh SHIT, I've completely blown this whole book. That's really typical. I might as well not have bothered. I should have known it was going to end up being lousy just because it was me doing it. The whole thing was a complete waste of time, just as I expected. That's really great, that is . . .

The End

OGRAPHIES

Well, that's the end of this *Book of the Dead*.

Every really serious book has lots of lists and ographies at the back, to prove how much heavy reading and research had to be done before the book could be written so here is all my source material and references and things that went into this book.

Really I put a lot of myself in this book so it was a bit difficult to know where to stop making lists.

Titleography

Here are some of the titles I thought about before going for
Neil's Book of the Dead:

1. *Neil's Official Good Hippy Guide 1984*
2. *The Totally Self-Sufficient Whole Earth Acoustic Holistic Alternative World Catalogue.*
3. *The Young Ones* by Neil
4. *The Duvet Snatchers*
5. *All you Need is Lentils*

Bibliography

The bibles I had to read before starting this book.
Every book has a bibliography but I don't see why on earth writers should have to read lots of bibles before they start writing. Completely mad! Anyway it's very difficult to tell what is a bible or what isn't. I mean someone told me that *Wisden's* is the cricketer's bible so I just read it to be on the safe side. I've probably read lots of other bibles without knowing it but here's a list anyway:

1. *Wisden's*, the cricketer's bible.
2. *Glass's Guide to Motor Vehicle Prices*, the second-hand car salesman's bible.
3. *Nobody Gets Out of Here Alive*, the Doors fan's bible.
4. *The Bible*, Cliff Richard's bible.

Drugography

These are the drugs that went into the making of this book (not including the bit of grass, tobacco and ashes between pages 22 and 23 which is just a mistake because someone must have used my *Book of the Dead* to roll a joint on).

1. Well, as far as drugs go, in these days of Thatcher and nuclear pollution, it's nice to know that pigeon shit roasted in an old shoe polish tin still works.

2. In fact, most of the things you can buy in a pet shop will do something funny to your head. However, *always* dry out gold fish fins thoroughly before smoking them.

3. There are plenty of other places to go and get completely zonked. For instance, the *laundry bag* when it's got really full towards the end of the month and it's sitting, waiting to go to the launderette – try opening the top of the bag quickly and sticking your face in. Inhale deeply and close the bag tight to stop any fumes getting out. Repeat this until you're feeling really heady or you pass out.

4. Other good places to sniff are around the kitchen sink or behind the toilet. But the most amazing turn-on is the one you get when you drape a towel over your head and kneel over the cat-lit. This one can make you feel really heavy for days.

5. And don't forget that some of the best trips can be self-sufficient. After you've had a take-away, go under your duvet, get into your flatulantra position and wave the duvet up and down vigorously as you breathe in the heady blast. *Warning* – leave it for a few days before repeating this process since black-outs have been known to occur.

Discography

These are the amazing sounds that have made me what I am today.

1. *The Lay of the Last Tinker* – Donovan
2. *The Smashing of Amps* – Jimi Hendrix
   (definitely better than *Purple Haze*)
3. *Ducks on a Pond Cousin Caterpillar* – The Incredible String Band
4. *Strangely Strange But Oddly Normal* – Dr Strangely Strange
5. *Hurdy Gurdy Man* – Steve Hillage
   (The only version)
6. *Hole in My Shoe* – Traffic

7. *Leaf and Stream* – Wishbone Ash
8. *Enigmatic Insomnia Machine* – Principal Edward's Magic Theatre
9. *Moonchild, The Dream, The Illusion* – King Crimson
10. *My Goal's Beyond* – Mahavishnu Orchestra
11. *We Love You* – Rolling Stones
    (The only good thing they ever did)
12. *Yeah! Heavy and a Bottle of Bread* – Bob Dylan
13. *Ghetto Raga* – Third Ear Band
14. *Bliss Trip (It's All The Same)* – Quintessence
15. *We're All Going to the Zoo Tomorrow* – Julie Felix
16. *Metal Guru* – T Rex
17. *The Faster We Go the Rounder We Get* – Grateful Dead
18. *Warm Heart Pastry* – Mike Heron
19. *The Beat Goes On* – Vanilla Fudge
20. *Everyone's Gone to the Moon* – Jonathan King
21. *Quite Rightly So* – Procol Harum
22. *The Teddy Bears' Picnic* – Henry Hall
23. *People Are Strange* (yeah, and don't I know it) – Doors
24. *Show Me the Way to Get Stoned* – David Peel and the Lower East Side
25. *Uncle Harry's Last Freak Out* – Pink Fairies
26. *Isn't Life Strange?* – Moody Blues
27. *Puff the Magic Dragon* – Peter, Paul and Mary
28. *Bombay Calling* – It's a Beautiful Day
29. *Oh Very Young* – Cat Stevens
30. *Thanks for the Pepperoni* – George Harrison

This is my Satanic Top 666 (i.e. an evil vibe in every groove).

1. *Money Money Money* – Abba
2. *Money* – Beatles
3. *Money* – Pink Floyd
4. *Money* – Flying Lizards
5. *Money Makes the World Go Round* – from *Cabaret*
6. *Tie a Yellow Ribbon Round the Old Oak Tree* – the famous Freemasons' anthem.

▼

Missedoutonography

Here are some things that I've really missed out on and resent. They're not in this *Book of the Dead* and haven't helped me in any way at all.

1. A Zorro outfit.
2. Anybody taking me seriously. Ever.
3. A major part in a James Bond movie.
4. Candy floss.
5. A pierced ear.
6. Any Topsy and Tim book.
7. A sewing basket.
8. A Tiny Tears Doll ('Once you pick her up, you'll never put her down').
9. A nurse's outfit.
10. A really complete full make-up set with nail-varnish and two-colour mascara.

Bookography

I didn't read many of these books but I've heard a lot of people talking about them.

1. *The Suzuki Book of Motorcycle Maintenance*
I did read this one and frankly it's a total rip-off. There's *not one* reference to Zen throughout and it's all about digital carburettors. If this is an underground bestseller, it can stay down there for all I care.

2. J. R. R. Tolkien, *Farmer Giles of Ham*
It contains all the essential wisdom, mythic folk-lore etc etc of *Lord of the Rings* but is only a few pages long so it's much easier to finish. Recommended.

3. Jerry Rubin, *Steal This Book*
This should have been called *Forget This Book*. I did what the title said and ended up having a really heavy discussion with the guy in my local head bookshop about the concept of private property in a capitalist society. He refused to let me steal it so I left a big bogey in it instead. I may not have the book but I think I made my point anyway.

4. Adam Gottlieb, *Legal Highs*
Lots of different ways of getting blasted in a totally organic way. Unfortunately my copy had a blank page so that something I took which Adam Gottlieb said was going to be harmless put me into a death-like trance. Contains the heavy philosophical

statement, 'STAY HIGH – STAY FREE!' Well, that's all very well, Adam, if you're getting big advances from alternative publishers.

5. *The Tibetan Book of the Dead*
More boring, more expensive, more depressing than this *Book of the Dead* with not nearly as many pictures.

6. Richard Neville, *Playpower*
I looked at this book and it was all about people I'd never heard of trying to get it together with under-age girls. Not recommended.

8. Kahlil Gibran, *The Prophet*
A very nice book, just the right shape, not much longer than *Farmer Giles of Ham* and famous for having a beautiful thought in every line. I'm opening my copy now. It says, 'Pity the stags cannot teach swiftness to the turtles.' See?

9. T. C. McLuhan, *Touch the Earth*
Not about the Pope like you might think but all nice pictures of Red Indians and some of the heavy things they said.

10. R. D. Laing, *Knots*
The heaviest kind of mindbenders for freaky intellectual wankers. R. D. Laing also invented lateral thinking, the naked ape and the female eunuch.

11. *Alternative England and Wales*
Oh no, this is another bible that I left out of my bibliography. It's a bible for anyone who wants to do anything anywhere – like having a religious experience, going to a VD clinic, making a teepee, sticking your tongue out at the pigs, telephoning America without paying, making a living out of selling your blood, joining a squat, cutting your own hair, tuning your guitar without a piano, hitching round the world, taking drugs, setting up your own crêche, publishing your own book . . . Oh shit, that sounds just like this book – why is it whenever I get an idea, someone goes and does it first?

Hassleography

Here are just some of the hassles that happened to me while writing this book, and the people that tried to stop me. And yet I finished it. That says something about me, right?

1. The guys.
2. Rik flushing the first draft down the toilet so I had to start again.

3. All the newsagents in our area ganging up on me and refusing to sell me biros.

4. Running out of toilet paper.

5. Rik using the second draft as toilet paper.

6. Running out of ideas on about page 14.

7. Vyvyan finding the third draft and showing it to all his friends and all of them laughing at me and making me eat it.

8. Getting constipated and having to wait a month to get over my writer's block so that I could start the fourth draft.

15. Getting interrupted by calls from a literary agent who was told by Mike I had a big one in the pipe-line and was I looking for someone to handle it.

16. Going through a whole identity crisis about whether it was me that really wrote the book, or was it some other Neil who took over? Of course, it was you, you jerk. Shit, who said that? Oh no, this is getting freaky now. I think writing's really bad karma.

17. Leaving the whole thing on the 78 bus by mistake.

Film and TVography

I do not watch violent fantasy cartoons like Tom and Jerry. Because *some* people happen to think it's not funny if a cat's tail gets flattened by a brick then singed by a hot iron before a whole bookshelf falls on it and squashes it flat and then the mouse comes along with a frying pan and starts tossing it in the air and it comes down in boiling fat and leaps out, hits its head on a branch and is catapulted towards a barn and – UH-OH! – the barn door's closed – SPERLAAAT!!! And the cat slowly slides down the door and shatters and crumbles into a thousand pieces. Imagine if that happened to you, right? Or even to someone you know. We'd soon see if you were laughing then.

And the same thing goes for *It's a Knockout* and *Game For a Laugh – Game for a Totally Agressive Meat-Eating Sneer* is what I call it.

As for films, these are the only ones worth seeing.

1. *Fantasia* (except for Mickey Mouse).

2. *Easy Rider* (except for the motorcycle bits).

3. *2001* (see it thirty times and you'll begin to see its significance).

4. *The Magnificent Seven*.

5. *Woodstock*.

Magazineography

Here are just some of the magazines I have read, ripped off, or otherwise used to fill up space in my *Book of the Dead*.

1. *International Times*
2. *Nasty Tales*
3. *OZ*
4. *My Own Way*
5. *Friends*
6. *I Like You*
7. *Rolling Stone*
8. *East Village Other*
9. *Beano*
10. *Ink*
11. *Berkeley Barb*
12. *Other Scenes*
13. *Gandalf's Garden*

Listography

You'll realise by now how incredibly interesting lists can be. Here are some of the lists that were going to go into this list section before my hand started aching.

1. My favourite shopping list.
2. A list of people I really dislike a lot.
3. Radiography. A list of all the x rays I've ever had.
4. A list of some of the best poos I've ever done (like the one that wouldn't go away when I flushed and had to be broken up with a mallet).
5. List of all the other things I could have done if I wasn't writing this book.
6. Pornography. A list of all the people I've almost gone to bed with.

Stupidography

No, this ography idea is getting really out of hand now. Who's interested in the stupid things I had to do to make this book? Anyway, I didn't do anything really stupid (unless you count sellotaping my toenail clippings to the roof of my mouth).

Peopleography

Nobody helped me with this book. I did it all myself, every single bit.
But since I've got a page to spare, here are some people who'd give me a heavy time if I didn't mention them:

(printer: make it really small type, okay?)

Design and sunshine:
Kate Hepburn, assisted by Fiona Doulton

Illustrations:
Kate Hepburn, Fiona Doulton,
Claudio Muñoz (Wayne sequence), Joseph Wright (Dream Power).

Photographs:
Mike Busselle (Bobos, T'ai Chi, Elf),
Caroline Blacker (Otling Fayre).

Beautiful editorial vibrations and picture research:
Linda Martin

Heavy straight publisher act:
Colin Webb

*Interfering bastards without whom
this would have been a really good book:*
Caroline Blacker, Malcolm Bowden, Ben Elton, Roberta Green,
Deborah Hopewell, Paul Jackson, Mark Lucas,
Rik Mayall, Lise Mayer, Alexei and Linda Sayle,
Maureen Vincent.

Totally patronising assistance in research:
Richard Adams, Simon Brint, Don Grant, Andy Nickolds,
Roger Planer, Roland Rivron, Kipper Williams, the British
Library, the Colindale Newspaper Library, the University
College Library.

People who behave like deadlines really mattered:
Barry and John at Diagraphic Typesetters,
Fred at Michael Dyer Associates.

Breadheads who hit me for credits and a lot of money:
Photographs: London Features International (Mama Cass,
Jim Morrison, George Harrison, John Peel, Leonard Cohen).
Radio Times Hulton Picture Library (Marc Bolan, Leonard
Cohen). Retna Ltd/David McGough (Mick Jagger)
Rex Features (Timothy Leary, John Peel). Topham Picture
Library (Elvis Presley, Timothy Leary, Germaine Greer,
Jerry Rubin, Peter Fonda).
Words: ATV Music for the lines from George Harrison's
It's All Too Much, Jonathan Cape Ltd for the extract from
Leonard Cohen's *Beautiful Losers*.